BRIDGES TO KNOWLEDGE
IN POLITICAL SCIENCE:
A HANDBOOK FOR RESEARCH

BRIDGES TO KNOWLEDGE IN POLITICAL SCIENCE: A HANDBOOK FOR RESEARCH

Carl Kalvelage
Minot State College

Albert P. Melone
Southern Illinois University
at Carbondale

Morley Segal
The American University

Palisades Publishers
Pacific Palisades, California

Library of Congress Catalog Card Number 84–061061

International Standard Book Number 0–913530–37–9

Cover photographs: Thomas Jefferson Building, The Library of Congress

Library of Congress Cataloging in Publication Data:

Kalvelage, Carl.
  Bridges to knowledge in political science.

  Bibliography: p. 22
  Includes index.
  1. Political science—Research.   I. Melone, Albert P.
II. Segal, Morley.   III. Title.
JA86.K34   1984   320'.072   84–61061
ISBN 0–913530–37–9

Palisades Publishers
PO Box 744, Pacific Palisades, Calif. 90272-0744

Printed in the United States of America

*Dedicated to the memory of
three educators who understood
the relationship between research and
teaching—John Bollens,
Donald Bruce Johnson, and Joseph Tanenhaus*

Contents

Preface

This book has been written with two goals in mind. First, experience teaches that students need a practical guide to sources in political science. Particularly in the last two decades, there has been an explosion of available materials and students need assistance in making the mass of material "user friendly." With this guide we hope they will discover that the magic and mystery often associated with producing term papers can give way to a more rational and effective approach. Second, students need instruction on how to conceptualize, research and write assigned papers. Instructors are sometimes amazed, perplexed and even offended when students ask: "Where do I begin?" Indolence is not the sole explanation for such queries. The fact is that too many students have never been instructed in the fine art of paper writing and, sadly, some have never been asked nor will ever be challenged to experience the joy of research. We hope this book will encourage students to undertake such projects and also provide educators with a handy aid in that instruction. No liberal arts education is complete without numerous and varied research writing experiences.

Rather than organizing the material around the logic of the library, we have organized the sources according to the steps a student must go through in developing a paper. Chapter 1 outlines our approach and presents a series of logical steps by which a student can survey basic sources in order to develop a topic. We believe that most sources can be used both as a source in and of itself as well as a springboard for further ideas and investigations. The bulk of the book contains numerous library sources divided into a number of functional categories. Studying the detailed Table of Contents will help readers focus upon particular materials quickly and with relative ease. There is a complete chapter on footnoting and bibliographic citations. We have included a discussion of the logic of citations as well as numerous examples both in the traditional format and the popular scientific notation style. The last chapter contains tips on additional student skills and other relevant instruction.

It should be realized that some of the annotated sources will not be the most up-to-date editions available. Many are regularly revised and re-issued most often under new editions, and sometimes under new titles. This is no cause for alarm. If one learns from this book as the authors intend, then locating the most up-to-date sources will be an easy matter. Hopefully, students will be introduced to this book in their freshman year and find it a useful learning tool throughout their college years, including graduate school and beyond. In fact, we recommend this book for all introductory courses at the undergraduate and graduate levels.

This book is itself a successor volume to two earlier versions published by General Learning Press under the title, *Research Guide in Political Science.* Because the contents have been sufficiently changed and a new author has been added it is believed that the new title is merited. It is hoped that the many instructors from around the country who adopted for classroom use the earlier title will find the latest effort at least as useful if not more so than earlier versions. We thank those instructors who took the time to offer suggestions for changes based upon their classroom experiences.

Although we are singularly accountable for any errors found within, the authors are not solely responsible for this volume. A task of this scope necessarily involves a host of others who have aided in conscious and unconscious ways. Two reference librarians have been particularly helpful through the years. Kay Schmidt, Chief of Reference Services at the American University Library, and James W. Fox of the Morris Library at Southern Illinois University have been most gracious in sharing their knowledge with us. A parade of graduate students at Southern Illinois University have been pressed into service to verify references and to check copy. They include: James Okoro, Carol Leach, Cass Van Der Meer, Jeffrey Jones, and Frances Lamendola. Sandy Hickam and Peggy Melone typed bits and pieces of the manuscript over a two year period, and the academically talented Ann Melone sat attentively checking sources while her father read aloud from galley proofs. Finally, we gratefully acknowledge the patience, good will, and strength of Virgene Bollens of Palisades Publishers for seeing this project through to completion.

C.K.
A.P.M.
M.S.

BRIDGES TO KNOWLEDGE
IN POLITICAL SCIENCE:
A HANDBOOK FOR RESEARCH

1

The Research Paper: Crisis or Opportunity

The Chinese symbol for crisis is also the symbol for opportunity. For many political science students the assigned research paper is experienced as both a crisis and an opportunity. This paper has persisted over the years as a significant part of college courses.

For the student it is an opportunity to:

pursue a topic or approach of one's own choosing

establish one's own focus boundaries and approach to a particular topic

identify and explore a variety of available sources

develop and utilize skills in critical thinking as one develops and tests hypotheses

develop and utilize skills in written expression as one pulls information together

experience the satisfaction of developing a unique and individual product

For the professor it is an opportunity to:

identify the topics in one's field which are currently most interesting to students

help the student develop skills in identifying information, critical thinking and written expression

evaluate the student on the basis of an independent project of his or her own choosing and implementation

Unfortunately what starts out as an opportunity for many students is soon experienced as a crisis. The most common problems in an assigned research paper are:

finding a topic which is both interesting and appropriate

narrowing the topic so that it is doable

knowing how and when to document and footnote

pulling research together and presenting it in an understandable form

This guide is designed to help the student avoid crises and take advantage of the opportunity presented by such papers. This chapter deals with the process by selecting and refining a topic into a testable proposition. It also presents a framework for dealing with the overwhelming array of information now available. Chapters two, three and four survey the available information sources in terms of that model. Chapter five deals with the thorny problems of footnotes, how to footnote and the even more difficult question of when to footnote. The final chapter deals with study skills and special areas of communication which are often troublesome to students—writing a letter to the editor, corresponding with government officials, developing a book report, marking books and interviewing political elites.

A PRACTICAL FORM FOR SELECTING A TOPIC

Selecting an initial topic can be time-consuming and frustrating. The problem is one of developing a focus which is both interesting and workable. Hours may be spent trying to formulate an approach or to research an unworkable topic. A topic that may be interesting ("How to Prevent World War III") is not always manageable; that which may be manageable ("Bolivia and American Tin Quotas") might not stir the imagination.

It is important to select a topic that is interesting as it is originally conceived and which will continue to hold interest throughout the difficult period of research. Choosing a topic and scanning the sources are not separate tasks; they are entwined—doing one helps the other. This section, therefore, concentrates on three important steps in developing an interesting and workable topic.

The first step in developing any formula is to define its elements. Thus, one must first decide upon an initial area. To simplify this process, possible research areas have been divided into two basic groups: the *concrete* and the *abstract*. These two general areas are further divided into subgroups.

To those who have no hint of even a possible topic, we suggest that you browse through several of the following:

Alternative Press Index
Congressional Quarterly
Facts on File: World News Digest
Foreign Affairs Bibliography
National Party Platforms
Public Affairs Information Service Index
Washington Information Directory

THE CONCRETE—BROWSING FOR IDEAS

There is a natural appeal to a concrete topic—that is, a topic concerned with a person, an entity or organization, an event, or a law. If one has a predisposition to investigate something, it is likely to be one of the above concrete items. If the idea of such a topic is appealing but it is difficult to choose the person or country which would be most interesting, creative browsing may be rewarding. Simply thumbing through several of the resources listed on the following pages may suggest several topics. For convenience, these sources have been divided into four groups:

Persons

Entities (which include the whole range of human organizations from nations to neighborhood groups)

Events

Laws, programs, and policies

The most useful and general of these groups are listed in a separate section followed by the more specialized sources. In most cases the title will give a general description of the work. For a more detailed description as well as the bibliographic citation, refer to chapters 3, 4, and 5.

A Person

The best general sources:
Biography Index (note topical index in each volume)
Congressional Quarterly Service
Encyclopedias and Yearbooks
Dictionary of American Biography
Who Said What?
The more specialized sources:
Citizens Look at Congress
Congressional Directory
Dictionary of American Biography
Facts about the Presidents
International Encyclopedia of the Social Sciences
Vital Speeches of the Day
McGraw-Hill Encyclopedia of World Biography

An Entity or Organization

The best general sources:
Almanac of American Politics
Encyclopedia of Nations
United States Government Manual
Worldmark Encyclopedia of Nations
Yearbook of International Organizations
The more specialized sources:
Encyclopedias and Yearbooks
Everyman's United Nations

Political Parties and Civic Action Groups
Municipal Yearbook
Yearbook of the United Nations

Events

The best general sources:
Congress and the Nation
Congressional Quarterly Service
An Encyclopedia of World History
Facts on File: World News Digest
National Journal
The more specialized sources:
America Votes
The Annual Register of World Events
Foreign Affairs Bibliography
Guide to American Foreign Relations Since 1700
New York Times Index
The Vietnam Conflict
World Almanac and Book of Facts

Laws, Policies, and Programs

The best general sources:
American Politics Yearbook
Congressional Information Service Index
Congressional Quarterly Service
National Party Platforms
Subject Guide to Major Government Publications
Yearbook of the United States
The more specialized sources:
The Constitution and What it Means Today
Everyman's United Nations
Gallup Opinion Index
Municipal Yearbook
Public Affairs Information Service Index
United States Government Manual
Vital Speeches of the Day
Weekly Compilation of Presidential Documents

THE ABSTRACT—BROWSING FOR IDEAS

Ideas and abstractions have been used for centuries to inspire, analyze and critique political action. We will view such concepts as:

1. *Values:* ideas and concepts implying desirability
2. *Problems:* ideas and concepts implying undesirability
3. *Process:* ideas and concepts that imply neither desirability nor undesirability

To be more explicit, *value* refers to any concept or idea that describes an interest, pleasure, moral obligation, desire, want, or need. It may refer to a measurable activity, like equal opportunity in employment, or to an intangible, such as "support for the regime."

Problem, the second organization classification, may also refer to a measurable activity or a feeling, but it is generally regarded as undesirable, such as a feeling of political alienation or apathy.

Process has no connotation of desirability or undesirability but simply refers to any observable or definable pattern in activities of people and groups. *Political process* refers to the pattern that emerges from the behavior of people and groups as they strive for and use political power.

Many ideas or concepts can be placed in two or even all three of these categories—depending upon the intent of the holder. Ronald Reagan's 1980 conservative sweep, for instance, can be treated as a desirable reversal of liberalism, a neutral process, or a tragic mistake. How one regards these ideas depends upon one's own attitudes. The categories of value, problem, and process simply help in identifying one's own feelings toward these ideas in order to use them in organizing a paper.

All three abstract concept classifications have one thing in common: as ideas, they cannot be seen, heard, or felt. Often they are not even recognized by those involved but are abstractions, imposed upon them by an outside observer. For example, look at the process of a group of grade school children saluting the flag. Neither these children nor their teacher may realize that they are involved in the "process of political socialization," but they would be observed as such by many political scientists.

Whatever one's preference for political description, these three categories of abstract ideas will be invaluable for organizing thoughts and ideas into a paper. Since most source books deal with ideas and concepts applicable to all three categories, they have been listed together. If a research source is especially relevant to one category, this has been indicated in parentheses.

Abstractions: values, problems and process

The best general sources:
ABS Guide to Recent Publications in the Social and Behavioral Sciences (process)
A Cross Polity Survey
Academic Journals
Editorial Research Reports
International Encyclopedia of Social Sciences

Masterpieces of World Philosophy in Summary Form
Public Affairs Information Service Index (especially for problems)
Safire's Political Dictionary
Social Sciences Index
The Syntopicon Volumes
Vital Speeches of the Day
The more specialized sources:
Congress and the Nation
Congressional Quarterly Service
The Constitution and What it Means Today
Essay on General Literature Index
Foreign Affairs Bibliography
National Party Platforms (problems)
Readers' Guide to Periodical Literature
Subject Guide to Major Government Publications
Weekly Compilation of Presidential Documents

As one begins to explore the material, it is usually discovered that far more has been written on the chosen topic than expected. The traditional advice is to "narrow" the topic, but this is only a partial answer, for "narrowing" in the traditional way can squeeze the life out of an interesting topic. The next section demonstrates how to narrow a topic and still keep it interesting.

DEVELOPING A TOPIC

"Narrow down your topic" is a common refrain of instructors when advising students. What is being called for is an intellectual process of reducing a topic in terms of either time or space. For example, instead of writing about Menachem Begin's entire life, the topic may be reduced to the years he spent as a terrorist fighting against the British presence in Palestine. Instead of writing about Canadian politics in general, a paper on the French speaking separatist movement might be developed.

The goal of the admonition to narrow down one's topic is to make the research project manageable. However, even then one may still find that there is far more written about the separatist movement or about Begin's terrorist past, for example, than can be studied reasonably within the span of the academic term. Thus, it is often necessary to refine the research topic until the project can be completed in a satisfactory manner given the constraints of time and energy. It is nonetheless important to guard against erring in the opposite direction; when a topic is finally narrowed down, it may be so limited in scope that it becomes a major task to even state the title!

Be cognizant of the choices made throughout the narrowing down process. Self-awareness can avoid the frustrations associated with either too much to write in too little time and space, or too little to say in so many required pages.

The legitimate goal in developing a topic is to focus clearly on interesting and worthwhile queries that might be answered. These are questions or problems that will help define what is and what is not an appropriate research topic. One way to accomplish this task is to combine the categories of the abstract and the concrete; for example, the topic of Martin Luther King (concrete) and the idea of "equality" (an abstract idea). There are a great many possible combinations of these categories. To help in identifying some of the possibilities for a topic, three charts have been constructed:

1. Combining the concrete and the abstract;
2. Combining one abstraction with another; and
3. Combining two or more concrete objects on the basis of an abstraction.

Tables 1, 2, and 3 illustrates these possibilities.

DEVELOPING A HYPOTHESIS

Topics provide a subject focus (Political Parties and Nomination of Women on the Federal Bench).

A hypothesis is a declaratory statement that purports to answer a question or a problem—(if there is a change in political party control of the White

TABLE 1-1: COMBINING THE CONCRETE AND THE ABSTRACT

	Process	Problem	Value
Person	The Moral Majority fundraising activities and the role of Senator Jesse Helms	Political violence as a tool of regime stability as employed by President Marcos of the Philippines	Nonviolence as a political statement and the life of Henry David Thoreau
Event	The procedures of UN Security Council in response to the mid-air destruction of a Korean civilian airliner by the Soviet Union	Religious preferences in voting and the 1960 presidential election	Congressional authority in matters of war and peace and the war in Vietnam
Entity	Lobbying in Congress and role of the Business Council	The reduction of political patronage and the breakdown of the Democratic political machine in Chicago	Political participation of older Americans and the Gray Panther Party
Law or Policy	Military aid to Lebanon and the War Powers Act	Searches of Rock-concert patrons, the Fourth Amendment and court decisions	International cooperation among nation-states and the NASA Space Shuttle program

TABLE 1-2: COMBINING TWO ABSTRACTIONS AS A FOCUS

	Process	Problem	Value
Process	The conflict between the doctrine of majority rule and the principle of judicial review of legislation	Candidate independence from special interests and the financing of elections	The Prepie outlook as expressed in Doonsbury and learning political attitudes
Problem	Rule by an oligarchy and membership participation in decision-making in voluntary organizations	Foreign espionage and electronic surveillance of U.S. citizens	Free elections in developing third world nation-states and covert great power intervention
Value	Foreign aid appropriation process in Congress and the elimination of world hunger	Deployment of nuclear weapons and world disarmament	Racial equality and meritorious advancement: Problems in Affirmative Action programs

House then there will be a change in the proportion of women to men nominated to serve on the federal bench). The statement must be phrased in a precise manner expressing what the researcher expects to find in the real world. There can be no mistake as to the anticipated relationship among the variables because each term in the hypothesis is subject to clear definition.

A typical hypothesis may be put in the form of an if-then statement. If A occurs, then B will occur. A is the independent variable that accounts for, influences, or causes the behavior of B, the dependent variable. For example, you might hypothesize, "If there is a change in political party control of the White House, then there will be a change in the proportion of women to men nominated to serve on the federal bench." Note the hypothesis as stated suggests that a change in the independent variable (party) will produce a change in the dependent variable (women on the bench).

It is not necessary to always state the hypothesis in the if-then form, although it is a useful guide to keep in mind. The above hypothesis might be changed slightly to read that "Democratic presidents have a greater propensity than Republican chief executives to nominate a greater proportion of women to men to the federal judiciary." However the hypothesis might be worded, what is important to remember is that a hypothesis is a proposition subject to testing; the statement must be amendable to confirmation or its opposite, disconfirmation. The way this is accomplished is to state the hypothesis in a precise fashion being certain that each term can be defined with an empirical referent in the real world.

We suggest that you define your hypothesis as early in the research process as possible. Unfortunately however, creative thought such as developing a

TABLE 1-3: COMBINING TWO OR MORE CONCRETE OBJECTS OF STUDY ON THE BASIS OF AN ABSTRACTION

	Person	Event	Entity	Law or Policy
Person	Fidel Castro, V.I. Lenin, and George Washington as revolutionaries	The U.S. response to the Soviet destruction of an unarmed Korean airliner as a reflection of the personality of Ronald Reagan	Organized labor and the presidential candidacy of Walter Mondale: What Impact?	United Nations policy on independence for Namibia: The negotiating role of UN Secretary-General Javier Pérez de Cuéllar
Event	The Ayatullah Khomeini and the U.S. 1980 presidential election: foreign influence on domestic politics	A comparison of deviating presidential elections: 1952, 1956, 1968, and 1980?	The American Bar Association and the defeat of anti-trust legislation in the 1970s	The U.S. boycott of the 1980 Summer Olympics and the Soviet invasion of Afghanistan: Trading Athletes for Bullets
Entity	His Royal Highness Sobhuza II and the Kingdom of Swaziland: A Modern Anomaly	The election of Harold Washington as mayor of Chicago and the cooperation of the city council	West German and Australian federal systems: A Comparison	Fair Trial versus Free Press: Comparing U.S. and United Kingdom legal practices
Law or Policy	Secretary of Agriculture Block and the use of grain embargos as an international political weapon	Watergate and legislating against "dirty tricks"	The Council on Foreign Relations and the War in Vietnam: An Example of the Policy-Planning Process	Comparing states with capital punishment and those without the death penalty: Deterrence or Vengeance?

hypothesis does not always take place in orderly steps. It would be nice if one could neatly define a research project, then search the library for sources. More likely is the process in which you begin to define your project, search the literature, and as you see what is available, refine your topic. Sometimes this process occurs several times with the hypothesis becoming more precise, clearer and achievable each time. For this reason we are suggesting that as you complete your basic literature search, write the testable propositions as they occur to you. After you discover what is available, you can consider which proposition you actually wish to test.

AN OVERVIEW OF INFORMATION SOURCES

As you begin to survey the available information on your topic you may find the amount of available information to be overwhelming. In some ways an oversupply is as frustrating as having too little.

One way to cut the oversupply of material is to view it in terms of three basic steps. The sources outlined in this guide are arranged in terms of these steps.

STEP ONE. Find the bridge to the appropriate information. Chapter 2 outlines the most important bridges to political science information:

abstracts and digests
indexes to periodicals, books and documents
book reviews
bibliographies

Each one of these bridges has its own unique structure, with maps, road signs and a logical system of organization and access to information. Chapter 2 describes the bridges leading to specific material and the best methods for their use.

STEP TWO. Survey the information. Just as it is useful to read something about a foreign country before you visit it, it is also useful to have an overview of a large body of information before you become immersed in it. Chapters 2 and 3 present those sources which offer you such an overview:

encyclopedias
dictionaries and glossaries
annuals, almanacs, atlases and yearbooks
biographic material
handbooks, directories and guides

As every nation has its own culture and language, every subarea of political science information has its own language, logic, roadsigns and pattern of organization. Chapter 3a outlines and describes the many available surveys in order to identify the most useful ones for a particular topic.

STEP THREE. Identify original sources. Depending upon the focus of a paper, virtually any source of information can be considered original. For example, a paper focusing upon women's reaction to Ronald Reagan could use publications of various feminist groups as original sources. Chapter 4 focuses upon three important sources of original data which are often underutilized by political science students:

government documents
data sources, polls and quantitative applications
academic journals

Each of these sources are underutilized for a different reason. Government documents are a rich source of vital information in political science but they are often hard to locate, decipher and document. This chapter outlines the basic guidelines needed to utilize local, state, national and international documents.

Data sources are also hard to locate for quantitative data can be found in books, special series of books and monographs, irregularly published periodicals and special computer packages. This chapter helps to identify and locate the most useful data packages for political scientists.

Academic journals, in contrast to government documents and data packages, are not hard to locate in most university libraries. This valuable source is often bypassed by students because they are not aware of which journal among the hundreds in most academic libraries is most relevant for their topic. This chapter helps to identify the particular focus of the most helpful academic journals.

MULTIPLE USES FOR INFORMATION SOURCES

These three steps are basic frameworks for classifying and utilizing the various types of information sources. However, they need not be restrictive. Almost any information source can be used in a variety of ways. For example, bridges to information can also be utilized to give you an overview of a body of information. A periodical listing or an index such as the *Environment Index* can also present a quick overview of the dimensions of a particular environmental policy area. As one example, a book review of a biography of Margaret Thatcher can provide a good overview of the issues involving her political leadership. Bridges to information can also be used as original sources. A paper on James Watts' press relations might use the index to the New York Times to document how coverage changed during the Reagan administration. Summaries such as encyclopedia articles also contain bibliographies and these can serve as useful first bridges to a body of information. Yearly reports in annuals can serve as original sources. The *Handbook of Political Behavior* can serve as an original source on a question of research methodology.

Original sources such as a congressional hearing might serve as the first bridge to the interest group involved in a particular public policy issue. A data sourcebook such as *American Social Attitudes Data Sourcebook 1947–1978* can serve to summarize various issues at a given time.

The following information sources can be used in a variety of ways. It is important for the student to use these three steps as basic guidelines and adapt information sources to the particular focus of an assignment.

2

Bridges to Information

Each one of the sources in this section serves as a bridge to a larger body of information. Some of these sources, such as the card catalog and general periodical indexes, connect with immense and unwieldy bodies of information. To use these sources effectively it is important to understand their internal system of organization and cross indexing of information.

Other sources lead toward more specialized types of information such as abstracts or book reviews. Others such as bibliographies guide toward specialized topics such as political terrorism. In all instances it is important to understand the strengths and limitations of whatever bridge is used. The following introductory comments and annotations will help to identify the most useful bridge to a particular topic and point out some of the advantages and pitfalls of each source.

2a THE CARD CATALOG—THE FIRST STEP

The card catalog is the first and primary bridge to information. It is especially useful because, unlike other guides, nothing will be listed there that your library does not have. Usually every book in the library will be listed on at least three cards:

1. Title card
2. Author card
3. Subject card (There may be several of these.)

Assuming that you do not know what specific book you are looking for, it is the subject card that will be of most help. The problem is to identify the subject. If it is a concrete subject, such as John F. Kennedy, you have no problem. Books about Kennedy will be identified by a typed subject heading over the title.

```
          KENNEDY, JOHN FITZGERALD, PRES. U.S., 1917–1963.
  E
  185.61   Brauer, Carl M       , 1946–
  .B7917      John F. Kennedy and the second reconstruction / Carl M. Brauer.
          New York: Columbia University Press, 1977. xi, 396 p. (Contemporary
          American history series)
          Bibliography: p. [367]–379.
          Includes index.

             1. Afro-Americans—Civil rights. 2. United States—Politics and gov-
          ernment—1961–1963. 3. Kennedy, John Fitzgerald, Pres. U.S., 1917–
          1963. I. Title

  DAU                                              EAUUsc    76–57686
```

If, however, your topic is a bit more abstract—"Kennedy and Afro-American Civil Rights," for example, you will have to take one figurative step back and decide what general process or subject you are dealing with and how this subject might be labeled in the card catalog.

In this instance, in addition to the listing under John F. Kennedy the card is also listed under a specific policy area — Afro-Americans—Civil Rights, and the more general category — United States—Politics and Government—1961–1963. These cross references are listed on the bottom of the cards.

```
          AFRO-AMERICANS—CIVIL RIGHTS
  E
  185.61   Brauer, Carl M       , 1946–
  .B7917      John F. Kennedy and the second reconstruction / Carl M. Brauer.
          New York : Columbia University Press, 1977.
             xi, 396 p. (Contemporary American history series)
          Bibliography: p. [367]–379.
          Includes index.

             1. Afro-Americans—Civil rights. 2. United States—Politics and gov-
          ernment—1961–1963. 3. Kennedy, John Fitzgerald, Pres. U.S., 1917–
          1963. I. Title

  DAU                                              EAUUsc    76–57686
```

The practical problem is to be able to identify the headings which would contain your card. This is especially true if your topic is more abstract as in the following book dealing with the influence of the media on public affairs.

ELECTIONS—UNITED STATES

PN
4888   MacKuen, Michael Bruce.
.P6   More than news : media power in public affairs / Michael Bruce Mac-
M3   kuen, Steven Lane Coombs ; foreword by Warren E. Miller. — Beverly
     Hills : Sage Publications, c1981.
        231 p. — (People and communication ; v. 12)
        Bibliography: 227–230.

        1. Press and politics—United States. 2. Journalism—Social aspects—
    United States. 3. Elections—United States.
    I. Coombs, Steven Lane. II. Title

DAU   EAUUsc   81–183

In this instance, the card can be found in three places.
1. Press and politics—United States
2. Journalism—Social Aspects—United States
3. Elections—United States
It is hard to be sure that you will be able to follow the same logic in categorizing your topic as the card catalog but there are several tactics which can help.
1. Ask yourself, "What is the general subject or process, and where is it taking place?" Example: Elections—U.S.
2. Find a card for one book even vaguely related to the subject and check the cross listings on the bottom of the card.
3. Consult the "See" and "See also" cards in the subject catalog.
4. Look at *Library of Congress Subject Headings* (Washington, D.C.: Library of Congress, 1980). This is a master list of subject headings. Look up what *you* are calling your subject, and the list will refer you to the *catalog* heading.
5. Ask the librarian.

2b ABSTRACTS AND DIGESTS

Abstracts are usually concise summaries of the main points of periodical literature and sometimes include other types of publications including books and speeches. Digests are closely related to abstracts and often the terms are employed interchangeably. However, digests tend to differ in that editors strive to arrange the summarized material with a more precise subject method in mind. For example, legal cases appear in the official court reports in chronological order, not according to topic or subject. A legal digest is a subject index to the reported cases which provides brief abstracts of the facts or holdings in a case. Both abstracts and digests offer a glimpse of the content of an article, book, data set, or judicial opinion to help decide whether the material should be tracked down and read. The number of abstracts in the political science field has grown dramatically in the last few decades. These research tools can save much time because a rapid survey of a topic can be conducted without actually searching out and reading the original materials. A scanning of specialized abstracts such as *Your Government and the Environment* can give a quick general grasp of the dimensions of the field.

American Digests. St. Paul, Minn.: West Publishing Company. Annual.

The *American Digest* is a colossal work consisting of over 327 volumes. It is a subject classification of all reported American law cases appearing in the West Publishing Company's National Reporter System. It digests cases from 1685 to the present. For a discussion of how to use this valuable legal tool see: Albert P. Melone and Carl Kalvelage, *Primer on Constitutional Law* (Pacific Palisades, Calif.: Palisades Publishers, 1982), pp. 13–17.

The American Political Process. Dwight L. Smith and Lloyd W. Garrison, eds. Santa Barbara, Calif.: ABC–Clio, 1972.

Contains incisive abstracts of key articles organized in refined categories. A characteristic article might list 20 article abstracts on ethnic voting in America.

American Statistics Index. Washington, D.C.: Congressional Information Service, 1972—.

A useful master guide and index to all statistical publications released by the U.S. government. This publication both indexes and abstracts statistical publications.

Current Digest of the Soviet Press. The American Association for the Advancement of Slavic Studies. Columbus, Ohio: Ohio State University, 1929—.

Next to being there, this publication is considered one of the best ways to study the Soviet Union. Published weekly, it contains American translations of all the major documents and significant articles from about 60 Soviet newspapers and magazines plus a complete index to the two principal dailies, *Pravda* and *Izvestia*. The translations are without comment or even interpretation but are excellent raw material for critical analysis. A detailed quarterly index is also published as is a new monthly, *Current Abstracts of the Soviet Press,* offering monthly highlights of Soviet news with emphasis on internal discussion.

Dissertation Abstracts International. Ann Arbor, Mich: University Microfilms, 1938—.

As a major source on doctoral dissertations in the United States, this publication offers a brief abstract of each paper, with emphasis on the methods and conclusions of the study. Available in both microfilm and full-size editions, it is compiled monthly.

Doctoral Dissertations in Political Science in Universities in the United States. Currently appearing in the fall issue of *P.S.*, the newsletter of the American Political Science Association, Washington, D.C.

Besides some dissertations not available from University Microfilms, this publication offers a list of dissertations in progress. Even though some are never completed, they can be excellent idea material.

Environment Abstracts. New York: Environment Information Center, 1974—.

While slanted toward scientific material, these abstracts, published monthly, enable the political science researcher to develop a grasp of the work in a specialized area.

International Political Science Abstracts. Oxford: Basil Blackwell, 1951–72; Paris: International Political Science Association, 1973—.

Prepared quarterly by the International Political Science Association and the International Studies Conference, with the support of the Coordination Committee on Documentation in the Social Sciences, each volume contains about 350 abstracts, including 150 abstracted journals. In the first volume, a very broad subject group is covered, with author and subject indexes. Subsequently, the arrangement is alphabetical by author, with cumulated subject and author indexes in the fourth issue of each year. Abstracts of articles in English are in English; those articles in other languages are translated into French only.

Peace Research Abstracts Journal. Clarkson, Ontario: Canadian Peace Research Institute, 1964—.

This monthly journal offers extensive abstracts of books and articles directly or remotely associated with peace. Its topical organization is useful for suggesting research ideas.

Political Science Abstracts. New York: Plenum, 1967—.

Formerly titled *Universal Reference System*. Political Science, Government and Public Policy Series. Princeton, N.J.: Princeton Research, 1969. This is a 10-volume set of references with annual supplements. It takes approximately 20 minutes to master the unique computerized index system of this source; once done, specialized high-quality bibliographies are available. Each of the volumes covers a major area of political science such as international affairs, legislative decision making, administrative management, law, jurisprudence, and judicial process. Each lists and summarizes thousands of books, articles, papers, and documents.

Poverty and Human Resources Abstracts. Ann Arbor: Institute of Labor and Industrial Relations, University of Michigan and Wayne State University, Sage, 1966—.

A bimonthly work containing abstracts of articles in such politically related areas as urban change, living standards, education, and housing.

Psychological Abstracts. Washington: American Psychological Association, 1927—.

Abstracts in the area of motivation, social psychology, group behavior, and other cross-disciplinary topics.

Sage Public Administration Abstracts. Beverly Hills, Calif.: Sage Publications, 1974—.

A useful research tool for students of public administration or public policy. Abstracts, books, articles, pamphlets, government publications, speeches, and other related materials.

Sage Urban Studies Abstracts. Beverly Hills, Calif.: Sage Publications, 1973—.

Abstracts, articles, books, and other research materials concerning all facets of urban life.

Sociological Abstracts. New York: Sociological Abstracts, 1952—.

In recent years many concepts and ideas in political science have come from sociology, with the idea of a social system originating with sociologist Talcott Parsons. Bureaucracy, socialization, public opinion, and many other "political" concepts are dealt with in sociological journals. These abstracts are divided into approximately 20 subsections and may be helpful in many areas.

Your Government and the Environment. Matthew J. Kerbec. Arlington, Va.: Output Systems, 1971—.

The environment issue is immensely complex. This guide pulls together the whole policy area with readable essays on such topics as pollution, changes in laws, new scientific findings, grant policies, and monitoring techniques. Loose-leaf supplements are provided each year.

2c ALMANACS, ANNUALS, ATLASES, YEARBOOKS

Almanacs are usually, but not always, annual publications containing a variety of useful factual information. The term *annual* refers to a serial publication which is issued once a year. A yearbook is also called an annual. Both contain current information which tends to change from one year to the next. Atlases are volumes of maps which may contain descriptive accompanying materials. All these almanacs, annuals, atlases, and yearbooks are extremely useful in locating current factual information in a rapidly changing political and social environment. Books and articles rarely contain current information; these must be updated by almanacs, annuals, atlases, and yearbooks. Term papers will reflect an up-to-date quality by consulting these valuable reference materials. Materials in this section tend either to emphasize facts and data such as the *World Almanac and Book of Facts,* or meaning and analysis, such as *The Yearbook of World Affairs.* Depending upon the disposition for gathering information, either of these types of book can help focus a topic.

The Almanac of American Politics. Michael Barone, Grant Ujifusa, and Douglas Matthews. Boston: Gambit, 1972—.
This biennial publication is the single best source on congressional districts and members of Congress. Much more than a statistical compilation, it provides a political analysis of each congressional district as well as data on key notes, group meetings of legislators, the census, federal spending, etc.

The Almanac of World Military Power. Trevor N. Dupuy, Grace P. Hayes, and John A. C. Andrews. San Rafael, Calif.: Presidio Press, 1980.
A biennial work that discusses the resources of nations as seen through military eyes. The authors consider all aspects of national power, location, economic power, and others as aspects of potential military power. Though most of this material is taken from public records, nowhere else is it assembled in this fashion. When a struggle breaks out somewhere on the globe, this source gives a ready assessment of each nation's potential strength.

American Jewish Year Book. Morris Fine, Milton Minnelfarb, and Martha Jelenko, eds. New York: American Jewish Committee, 1899/1900—.
With the emergence of the Israeli conflict, American Jews have become an especially active and influential group in American politics. This detailed book of essays deals with a wide spectrum of Jewish life in the United States and the world, covering civic, political, and communal issues.

Annual of Power and Conflict 1980-1981: A Survey of Political Instability and Violence, Its National and International Repercussions. 10th ed. Institute for the Study of Conflict. London: Institute for the Study of Conflict, 1981—.
An annual survey of political violence, subversion, and instability with discussions of the chronology of events and narrative analyses by region and nation state. The 1981 edition features regional introductions, country surveys, chronologies, and international agreements.

The Annual Register of World Events. London: Longmans, 1761—.
A British publication first edited by Edmund Burke that heavily emphasizes Great Britain and the Commonwealth in what is considered to be one of the best summaries of year-by-year events. It also covers political, economic, and cultural events and speeches from around the world, with summaries. The events—political and nonpolitical—are written in notable prose and are integrated into quarterly reports.

Canadian Annual Review of Politics and Public Affairs. John Saywell, ed. Toronto, Ont., and Buffalo, N.Y.: University of Toronto Press, 1960—.
Contains definitive essays on important aspects of Canadian government and politics. It covers Parliament, federal/provincial relations, the parties,

each province, external affairs, and the economy. It is a good first stop for a paper on Canada.

Compendium of Social Statistics. New York: United Nations, 1963—.
  (Annotated in Chapter 4a.)

County and City Data Book. U.S. Bureau of Census. Washington, D.C.: Government Printing Office, 1952—.
  (Annotated in Chapter 4e.)

A Cross Polity Survey. Arthur S. Banks and Robert Textor. Cambridge, Mass.; MIT Press, 1968.
  (Annotated in Chapter 4a.)

Current World Leaders: Speeches and Reports. South Pasadena, Calif.: Almanac of Current World Leaders, 1970.
  (Annotated in Chapter 3i.)

Demographic Yearbook. Statistical Office. New York: United Nations, 1948—.
  Offers detailed world figures on population, projected trends, etc.

The Europa Yearbook. London: Europa, 1959—.
  A comprehensive multi-volume collection of information about all the countries of the world, not just Europe. In addition, this work deals in great detail with international organizations. There is information on daily newspapers, radio and television stations, banking structures, religions, and institutions—all by specific name.

Freedom in the World: Political Rights and Civil Liberties, 1978—. Raymond D. Gastil. New York: Greenwood Press, 1981.
  Beginning in 1978, Freedom House in cooperation with two publishers, has produced yearbooks centering on its survey of freedom in the world. These surveys possess an obvious Western bias. Yet they provide comparative data on political and civil liberties for all the nations of the world. In addition to raw data, they contain essays and country surveys. These data can be valuable to students of comparative government and public law.

Historical Atlas. 9th ed. Revised and Updated. William Robert Shepherd. New York: Barnes & Noble, 1976.
  (Annotated in Chapter 3f.)

Historic Documents of (Year). Washington, D.C.: Congressional Quarterly, 1972—.

Brings together the important speeches, documents, and pronouncements from a particular year. It is especially useful to show how quickly the significance of various items can change (see, for example, Richard Nixon's comments on Watergate and the Democratic party platform on energy).

The International Almanac of Electoral History. Thomas Mackie and Richard Rose. New York: Facts on File, 1982.
    (Annotated in Chapter 4a.)

Issues Before the General Assembly. United Nations Association of the United States of America. New York: UNA–USA, 1972.
    Published annually, this gives a concise summary of the issues before the General Assembly each year.

New International Yearbook: A Compendium of the World's Affair. New York: Dodd, Mead and Co., 1970—.
    A reference work that charts the events and progress of the year, classifying each under such categories as politics, foreign affairs, labor, sports, etc. It is indexed and includes photographs, charts, and detailed statistics.

Political Science Annual: An International Review. Indianapolis, Ind.: Bobbs-Merrill, 1966—.
    Patterned after annual reviews of research that have flourished in the natural sciences for many years, these essays focus primarily on the discipline of political science and only secondarily on the political phenomenon being studied. The volumes are useful for advanced students who want to understand the state of the discipline at a particular time. Examples are conflicting conceptions of political violence, and American political parties, an interpretation with four analytic levels.

Public Policy, An Annual Yearbook. The John Fitzgerald Kennedy School of Government, Harvard University. Cambridge, Mass.: Harvard University Press, 1940—.
    Each issue contains scholarly articles about practical problems of wide topical range. This became the quarterly periodical *Public Policy* in 1969.

Research Annual on Intergroup Relations. Melvin Tumin and Barbara Anderson. New York: Quadrangle Books, 1966–70; Chicago: Quadrangle Book, 1970—.
    Many political conflicts are reflections of group conflicts—American racial and religious conflicts, Arab and Israeli conflicts, Catholics versus Protestants, conflicts of French- and English-speaking residents of Canada. This source presents brief abstracts of all the important research on intergroup conflict each year. Articles are grouped according to the type of conflict discussed—i.e., racial, religious, linguistic, etc.

Setting National Priorities, the Budget. Washington, D.C.: The Brookings Institution, 1971—.

The federal budget is the major blueprint for government policy, yet it is extremely confusing to lay people. This yearly guide analyzes the budget issue by issue. The chapter on defense, for example, identifies and explains the issues in defense spending—pay, manpower, type of weapons, military forces in Europe, etc. An excellent first source.

The Statesman's Yearbook: Statistical and Historical Annual of the States of the World. New York: St. Martin's Press, 1864—.

A great yearbook of more than general value, this book offers a yearly update of economic, political, and social statistics as well as information on international organizations and on every country functioning during the preceding year. The data include each nation's constitution, political and governmental structure, financial basis, gross national product, court system, etc.

Statistical Abstract for Latin America. Center of Latin American Studies. Los Angeles: University of California, 1955—.

(Annotated in Section 4a.)

United Nations Yearbook of National Accounts Statistics. New York: United Nations Statistical Office and Department of Economic and Social Affairs, 1958—.

(Annotated in Chapter 4a.)

World Almanac and Book of Facts. New York: Newspaper Enterprise Association, 1868—.

Published yearly, first by the *New York World-Telegram and Sun,* the *World Almanac* supplies a wealth of information in every area likely to be investigated. A random sample of the broad spectrum of work includes the latest sports records; Nobel Peace recipients; listings of colleges and universities; heads of states; brief descriptions of foreign countries; a list of United States art galleries; biographies of Presidents and their wives, cabinet members, Supreme Court judges, and ambassadors; and even directions for drawing up a proper will.

In the same category as the *World Almanac* and furnishing basically the same information are *Information Please Almanac* (New York: Simon & Schuster, 1955-); *Reader's Digest Almanac,* edited by *Reader's Digest* editors (New York: Funk & Wagnalls, 1966-); and *The Official Associated Press Almanac* (Maplewood, N.J.: Hammond, 1973-).

The Urban Affairs Annual Reviews. Beverly Hills, Calif.: Sage, 1967—.

These are yearbooks on practical matters of government and administration. Each volume focuses on a particular problem such as "Improving the

Quality of Urban Management." Authors tend to be administrators, consultants, or academicians with a problem-solving orientation.

Yearbook on Human Rights. New York: United Nations Department of Social Affairs, 1947—.

Describes constitutional, legislative, and legal developments in a large number of states and trust territories—all bearing on human rights.

Yearbook on International Communist Affairs. Milorad M. Drachkovitch. Stanford, Calif.: Hoover Institute, 1967—.

Contains articles on each country of the world by specialists on communist activity for that year.

Yearbook of International Organizations. Eyvind S. Tew, ed. Brussels, Belgium: Union of International Associations, 1948—.

Of the more than 2,000 international organizations listed herein, fewer than 50 are affiliated with the United Nations, a fact that gives many a scholar pause. Of course, those not carrying UN credentials do not often make the front pages, but in their particular areas, they are influential. Without a guide of this type, they would undoubtedly elude most students. Those organizations not carrying UN credentials include a range from the highly political International Peace Association to the relatively esoteric International Association of Art Critics. Each entry covers the general history and a description of the organization and, more important, direction to sources of further information.

Yearbook of the United Nations. New York: United Nations Department of Public Information, 1947—.

These annual editions constitute a year-by-year record of the activities of the United Nations. Each edition is designed to present, in a single, fully indexed volume, a compact authoritative account of the deliberations and actions of the United Nations as well as the activities of the intergovernmental agencies related to it.

The Yearbook of World Affairs 1978—. George W. Keeton and George Schwarzenberger, eds. Boulder, Colo.: Westview Press, 1978—.

Not a typical reference book reviewing the past year's events. Rather, each annual volume since 1978 contains articles of contemporary interest to students of international relations. It contains some bibliographical entries under the heading "Trends and Events." Examples of articles include: "OPEC and the World Economy," "The Making of Zimbabwe: From Illegal to Legal Independence," and "The Hostage Incident: The United States and Iran."

2d BIBLIOGRAPHIES

A bibliography is a list of publications on a given subject. If card catalogs could include subject listings for every important aspect of a book, booklet, magazine article, or other source, there would be no need for bibliographies. The fact is, however, that the subject listing is so broad that it is rare to find one precisely fitting a topic. Furthermore, there are probably important sources, such as periodicals, that are not listed in the card catalog. In such cases, the most helpful bridge is a bibliography. If the subject heading is known, bibliographies will be listed in the card catalog under that heading; if it is not known, the next best source for bibliographies is *Bibliographic Index* and the more specialized bibliographies listed below.

The best known use of a bibliography is that it leads to other information on a subject. The other less known use of a bibliography is that it is *itself* a source of information on a subject. At the beginning of research on a given subject, the bibliography is searched for:

1. The way it breaks down and organizes various topics.
   This in itself can help organize a paper.
2. The annotations or comments about each source.
3. The comments or analysis about the subject in general.

ABC POL SCI: A Bibliography of Contents: Political Science & Government. Santa Barbara, Calif.: American Bibliographical Center. CLIO Press, 1969—. (Annotated in Chapter 2f.)

ABS Guide to Recent Publications in the Social and Behavioral Sciences. Beverly Hills, Calif.: The American Behavioral Scientist, Sage, 1965—.
Drawing from more than 400 monthly publications in sociology, anthropology, psychology, public policy, and political science, this guide identifies the most interesting articles. The guide will identify new articles in areas such as the psychological reasons behind a particular voting trend. It contains monthly new studies citations from back issues of *American Behavioral Scientist* to nearly the end of 1964. Subsequent citations are in monthly *Am. Beh. Sci.* or in *ABS' New Studies* section, published separately each month.

African International Relations: An Annotated Bibliography. Mark W. DeLancy. Boulder, Colo.: Westview Press, 1981.
Most of the annotated books, journals, articles, and pamphlets were published between 1960 and 1978, although there are a few entries for earlier years and a few works published in 1979 and 1980. The entries are divided into 11 subject areas covering such topics as sub-continental regionalism and U.S. relations with Africa.

Alternatives in Print: An International Catalog of Books, Pamphlets, Periodicals and Audiovisual Materials. 6th ed. Compiled by American Library Association. New York: Neal-Schuman, 1980. Formerly listed as *Alternatives in Print; The Annual Catalogue of Social Change,* Compiled by American Library Association. Columbus, Ohio: Ohio State University Libraries, 1973.

A guide to a wide range of political movements and their publications. Organizations are indexed by subject, and each entry includes publications, price lists, and information for ordering.

American Constitutional Development. Alpheus T. Mason and D. Grier Stephenson, Jr., compilers. Arlington Heights, Il: AHM Publishing Corp., 1977.

A selective bibliography of books, articles and doctoral dissertations on American Constitutional history, politics and law. Works are arranged both historically and according to subject matter.

American Defense Policy Since 1945: A Preliminary Bibliography. John Greenwood, ed. National Security Education Program. Lawrence, Kan.: University Press of Kansas, 1973.

Contains more than 3,000 items with a detailed table of contents.

Amnesty in America: An Annotated Bibliography. Morris Sherman, Passaic, N.J.: New Jersey Library Association, 1974.

Citations go back to 1790 on all aspects of the amnesty question.

Attitude Change: A Review and Bibliography of Selected Research. Earl E. Davis. Paris: UNESCO, 1964.

An analytic bibliographic essay on the various kinds of research behind attitude change.

Bibliographic Index. New York: H. W. Wilson, 1937—.

This master source for bibliographies lists bibliographies published separately as well as those found in books, pamphlets, and periodicals. It is published semi-annually.

A Bibliography for the Study of African Politics. Robert B. Shaw and Richard L. Sklar. Los Angeles: Crossroads Press, 1977—. First published in 1973 as a monograph by African Studies Center, University of California, Los Angeles.

Today it contains nearly 4,000 entries from diverse sources.

The Catholic Left in Latin America: A Comprehensive Bibliography. Therrin C. Dahlin, Gary P. Gillu, and Mark L. Grover. Boston, Massachusetts: G. K. Hall & Co., 1981.

The Catholic Left movement is a fascinating development for anyone interested in the dynamics of change. This English and Spanish language bibliography is divided by topic under each Latin American country. Among the over 20 topics listed are: revolution, peasantry, and the Catholic church and social change.

Comparative Public Policy: A Cross-National Bibliography. Douglas E. Ashford, Peter J. Katzenstein, and T. J. Pempel. Beverly Hills, Calif.: Sage Publications, 1978.

A good beginning for those interested in the study of public policy from a comparative perspective. The authors identify eight policy areas and provide books and journal articles for five countries under each policy subject. The eight policy areas are: administrative reform, economic management, local and regional reorganization, labor relations, race and migration, social security, higher education, and science and technology. The five countries are: United States, Great Britain, France, West Germany, and Japan.

Confrontation, Conflict, and Dissent: A Bibliography of a Decade of Controversy, 1960-1970. Albert Jay Miller. Metuchen, N.J.: Scarecrow, 1972.

While not annotated, the citations are numerous and arranged in topical chapters, covering general information, student dissent, firearms, etc.

Evolution of the Modern Presidency: A Bibliographical Survey. Fred I. Greenstein, Larry Berman, Alvin S. Felzenberg with Doris Lidtke. Washington, D.C.: American Enterprise Institute for Public Policy Research, 1977.

Students researching the U.S. presidency from 1932 will find this reference work a great time saver. It contains about 2,500 bibliographical entries, a few hundred of which are annotated.

Foreign Affairs Bibliography: A Selected and Annotated List of Books on International Relations 1962-1972. Council on Foreign Affairs. New York: R. R. Bowker, 1976.

Actually a ready-made bibliography on even the most specialized foreign policy topics of the United States and other nations. Organized nation by nation as well as by topic, it contains such subheadings as liberalism, conservatism, colonial problems, labor movements, human rights, and the Cold War, and brief annotations that include books, research series, and documents.

Foreign Affairs 50 Year Bibliography: New Evaluations of Significant Books on International Relations 1920-1970. Byron Dexter, ed. Council on Foreign Relations. New York: R. R. Bowker, 1972.

Each decade the influential *Foreign Affairs* publishes important bibliographies and reviews books on world affairs. This is a reexamination of the best reviews and essays.

Free at Last: A Bibliography of Martin Luther King, Jr. William H. Fisher. Metuchen, N.J.: Scarecrow Press, Inc., 1977.

An annotated bibliography of books, articles, dissertations, and other materials by and about the most important civil rights figure of the century.

Guide to Public Administration. D. A. Cutchin. Itasca, Ill.: F. E. Peacock Publishers, Inc., 1981.
   (Annotated in Chapter 3a.)

Housing and Planning References. United States Department of Housing and Urban Development. Washington, D.C.: Government Printing Office, 1948—.
   (Annotated in Chapter 4c.)

Information Sources of Political Science. 3rd ed. Frederick L. Holler. Santa Barbara, Calif.: ABC-Clio, 1981.
   Unlike the previous editions, the 3rd edition is a one-volume reference work of comprehensive scope. It contains standard sources for political science reference documents containing 1,750 annotations describing books, periodicals, and other materials. This fine volume is subdivided into subject areas for easy reference.

Intelligence, Espionage, Counterespionage, and Covert Operations: A Guide to Informative Sources. Paul W. Blackstock, and Frank L. Schaf, Jr. Detroit: Gale Research Company, 1978.
   Contains critical annotations of books, government documents, and newspaper articles on practically every aspect of this topic of contemporary interest. Students seeking to update this bibliography should probably begin in 1976 working forward to the current date.

International Bibliography of Political Science. 9 vols. The International Committee for Social Sciences Documentation. Chicago: Aldine, 1952–76; Paris: UNESCO, vol. 9; London: Talstock Publications, 1977—.
   These annual volumes contain a select worldwide list of the most important books and articles in political science. The topics often are highly specialized.

International Organization: An Interdisciplinary Bibliography. Michael Haas. Stanford, Calif.: Hoover Institution Press, 1971.
   This work has approximately 8,000 entries covering international organizations from the Greek city-states to the present, regional government, proposals for world government, etc.

International Organizations: A Guide to Information Sources. Alexine Atherton. Detroit: Gale Research Co., 1976.
   (Annotated in Chapter 3b.)

International and Regional Politics in the Middle East and North Africa: A Guide to Information Sources. Ann Schulz. Detroit: Gale Research Co., 1977.
   (Annotated in Chapter 3b.)

The International Relations of Eastern Europe: A Guide to Information Sources. Robin Alison Remington. Detroit: Gale Research Co., 1978.
(Annotated in Chapter 3e.)

John F. Kennedy: An Annotated Bibliography. John I. Newcomb. Metuchen, NJ: The Scarecrow Press, 1977.
A fine annotated bibliography of books, articles, and other materials by and about President Kennedy.

The Literature of Isolationism: A Guide to Non-Interventionist Scholarship, 1930-1972. Justus D. Doenecke. Colorado Springs, Colo.: Ralph Myles, 1972.
In the form of an extensive bibliographical essay, this book covers scholarship suggesting that a nation (the United States) should remain uninvolved with the rest of the world.

Literature on Judicial Selection. Nancy Chinn and Larry Berkson. Chicago: The American Judicature Society, 1980.
An annotated bibliography of the literature on judicial selection published between 1913 and 1980. It is the most complete list of articles and books available on the subject.

The Literature of Terrorism: A Selectively Annotated Bibliography. Edward F. Mickol, compiler. Westport, Conn.: Greenwood Press, 1980.
A well indexed bibliography useful to any student interested in this field of study.

Nationalism and National Development: An Interdisciplinary Bibliography. Karl W. Deutsch and Richard L. Merritt. Cambridge, Mass.: MIT Press, 1970.
An extensive history plus an exhaustive index by author and key word in title.

Political Campaign Communication: A Bibliography and Guide to the Literature. Lynda Lee Kaid, Keith R. Sanders, and Robert O. Hirsch. Metuchen, N.J.: Scarecrow, 1974.
Includes entries relevant to the communications process as it operated in a political campaign or similar contest in the United States from 1950 to 1972. It is specialized, but the beginning student can easily become interested in such works as James Powell's "Reactions to John F. Kennedy's Delivery Skills in the 1960 Campaign," *Western Speech,* 1968.

Political Science Bibliographies. Robert B. Harmon. Metuchen, N.J.: Scarecrow, 1976.
Contains nearly 800 entries listing many bibliographies in the field.

Poverty in the United States During the Sixties. Dorothy Campbell Tompkins. Berkeley, Calif.: Institute of Government Studies, University of California, 1970.

The 1960s witnessed a "war on poverty." This huge volume outlines the massive research accompanying the anti-poverty effort. Arranged by topic with limited annotations, it is action oriented: Who are the poor? Where do they live? What is being done for them?

Primer on Constitutional Law. Albert P. Melone and Carl Kalvelage. Pacific Palisades, Calif.: Palisades Publishers, 1982.

Chapter 2 contains a survey of the book literature in the general field of constitutional law. The selected bibliography at the end of the book contains extensive lists of books in the field.

Public Administration in American Society: A Guide to Information Sources. John E. Rouse, Jr. Detroit, Michigan, Gale Research Co., 1980.

An excellent annotated bibliography touching upon almost every aspect of public administration. It is well indexed, providing multiple conceptual approaches to the subject matter.

Public Administration Moves Into the Eighties: A Bibliography and Survey of the Field. Howard E. McCurdy. 2d ed., New York: Marcel-Dekker, 1984.

Contains a thorough cross-disciplinary bibliography. Public administration is an applied field with roots in a number of academic disciplines. The survey filed is presented in the form of a map of the discipline, tracing the roots of public administration to its varied sources in sociology, psychology, and political science.

Public Policy: A Guide to Information Services. William J. Murin, Gerald Michael Greenfield, and John D. Buenker. Detroit: Gale Research, 1981.

Policy analysis is the most rapidly growing sub-field in political science. Topics covered include theories and concepts of public policy and decision making plus a variety of policy fields appropriate for term paper research, criminal justice, health, housing, science, etc. The sources are wide ranging and include both academic process-oriented pieces and specialized sources in each area. This book is as much a book about Congress itself as it is a guide to sources. It is a step-by-step guide in the use of the maze of paper produced in the legislative process. It describes how to trace legislation, how to research the legislative and political record of the legislators themselves including the characteristics of their district; an extremely useful first source on Congress.

The Role of Political Parties in Congress: A Bibliography and Research Guide. Charles O. Jones and Randall B. Ripley. Tucson: University of Arizona Press, 1966.

Although specialized and relatively short, this bibliography nevertheless serves as a guide, describing how to locate and use documents, subjects for study, etc.

The Secret Wars: A Guide to Sources in English. 3 volumes. Myron J. Smith, Jr. Santa Barbara, Calif.: ABC-Clio Press, 1980–81.

As part of the War/Peace Bibliography Series developed at the Center for the Study of Armament and Disarmament, California State University, Los Angeles, the author has organized the vast literature of secret or clandestine warfare into three volumes, each confined to a historical period. Volume I contains an extensive bibliography on the underground activity during World War II (1939–1945). Volume II contains references to the secret service operations of Western and Communist nations during the Cold War period, 1945–1950. And finally, Volume III contains good coverage of international terrorism, 1968–1980. Those investigating "secret wars" can save themselves considerable times by consulting this set which contains not only references to books, journal articles, government documents, and dissertations, but each volume provides chronologies of events and brief scholarly introductions to the subject matter.

A Selected Bibliography of American Constitutional History. Stephen M. Millett. Santa Barbara, Calif.: Clio Books, 1975.

An excellent bibliography covering every facet of constitutional history. Also contains a fine section on judicial biographies.

Selection of the Vice-President. Dorothy Campbell Tompkins. Berkeley, Calif.: Institute of Governmental Studies, University of California, 1974.

Includes history as well as quotations and suggestions for change.

State Government Reference Publications: An Annotated Bibliography. 2d ed. David W. Parish. Littleton, Colo.: Libraries Unlimited, Inc., 1981.

A common problem encountered in the study of state government is locating materials. While other source materials exist—most notably the U.S. Library of Congress *Monthly Checklist of State Publications—*, few furnish the depth of coverage and organization provided by David Parish. The book is divided into nine chapters: Official State Bibliography; Blue Books; Legislative Manuals and Related References; State Government Finances; Statistical Abstracts and Other Data Sources; Directories; Tourist Guides; Audiovisual Guides, Atlas, and Maps; Bibliographies; and General References. The existent state materials are arranged alphabetically within each of these chapters. The book also contains an excellent title, author and subject indexes.

The Study and Analysis of Black Politics: A Bibliography. Hanes Walton, Jr. Metuchen, N.J.: Scarecrow, 1973.

Contains useful introductory essays on the variety and scope of writings on the Black political experience. The extensive listings are not annotated but are arranged topically, i.e., Black political candidates, Black pressure groups, etc.

The Study of Community Power: A Bibliographic Review. Willis D. Hawley and James H. Svara. Santa Barbara, Calif.: ABC-Clio, 1972.

A bibliographic essay at its best. It emphasizes the theoretical and methodological issues involved in the study of community power and has extensive annotation.

Sub-Saharan Africa: A Guide to Information Sources. W. A. E. Skurnick. Detroit, Mich.: Gale Research Co., 1977.

Although some updating would be required, this annotated bibliography contains excellent references on: Pan-Africanism, Western Europe, and Africa, the U.S. and Africa, Socialist countries and Africa, and African Liberation movements. It also has an excellent chapter on reference works including government documents, handbooks, general bibliographies and bibliographic essays.

Suburbia: A Guide to Information Sources. Joseph Zikmund II and Deborah Ellis Dennis. Detroit, Mich.: Gale Research Co., 1979.

Anyone who has ever attempted to locate the literature on suburbia will welcome this most useful annotated bibliography. It is divided into a number of different conceptual and functional categories and contains appendexes directing researchers to bibliographies, abstracts, indexes, and periodicals.

The Supreme Court and the American Republic: An Annotated Bibliography. D. Grier Stephenson, Jr. New York: Garland Publishing Inc., 1981.

A fine bibliography of books and articles on all aspects of the U.S. Supreme Court and the Constitution. It includes brief annotations of leading court cases and difficult-to-locate biographical and autobiographical materials as well.

The United States Congress: A Bibliography. Robert A. Goehlert and John Sayre. New York: Free Press, 1982.

At the time of publication, this was the most thorough, up-to-date bibliography on U.S. Congress. It is not annotated but it is broken down into highly detailed subsections. For example, there is a subsection with 41 entries on the rights of witnesses before congressional committees. Such detailed organization can be very useful in focusing and researching a paper.

U.S. Constitution: A Guide to Information Sources. Earlean M. McCarrick. Detroit, Michigan, Gale Research Co., 1980.

A much welcomed annotated bibliography useful for political science and history students researching aspects of the U.S. Constitution. Early chapters are excellent treatments of books and articles dealing with events before and including constitutional ratification. The remainder is devoted to each branch of the national government, the federal system, and annotations on each amendment.

U.S. Foreign Relations: A Guide to Information Sources. Elmer Plischke. Detroit, Mich.: Gale Research Co., 1980.

Assigned a term paper on some aspect of U.S. foreign relations? This massive annotated bibliography is the place to start. It is a most complete treatment of the subject matter.

United States/Middle East Diplomatic Relations 1784-1978: An Annotated Bibliography. Thomas A. Bryson. Metuchen, N.J.: Scarecrow Press, Inc., 1979.

Includes annotations of books and articles arranged historically. It also lists doctoral dissertations on the subject.

U.S. Politics and Elections: A Guide to Information Sources. David J. Maurer. Detroit, Mich.: Gale Research Co., 1978.

An annotated bibliography of the book literature on U.S. politics and elections divided into historical periods dating from 1607 and ending in 1976. The last chapter is topical rather than historical and contains sections including "money and influence," "third parties and divergent politics," and "Negro politics." This bibliography makes no pretense at being complete, but it is an excellent source of the literature for particular historical periods.

Urban Environment and Human Behavior: An Annotated Bibliography. Gwen Bell, Edwina Randall, and Judith E. R. Roeder. Stroudsburg, Pa.: Dowden, Hutchinson, & Ross, 1973.

Solidly interdisciplinary and with extensive annotations, it emphasizes the psychological and sociological aspects of urban life, citizens planning, visual perceptions, aspects of space, etc.

Urban Management: A Guide to Information Sources. Bernard H. Ross. Detroit, Mich. Gale Research Co., 1979.

An interdisciplinary bibliography of the broad field of urban management. Annotations are incisive, and subject areas such as urban public interest and professional associations provide a focus usually not available to political scientists. An excellent first stop for any paper focusing on urban affairs.

Urban Policy: A Guide to Information Sources. Dennis J. Palumbo and George A. Taylor. Detroit, Mich.: Gale Research Co., 1979.

This is a partially annotated bibliography of books and periodical literature on various aspects of public policy as it pertains to the urban environment. Students of urban politics, public administration, and public policy will find this bibliography well organized and expertly indexed. The authors have concentrated on urban policy in the subject areas of education, transportation, criminal justice, housing, urban renewal, race, ethnicity, health, and poverty.

The Vietnam Conflict: Its Geographical Dimensions, Political Traumas, and Military Developments. Milton Leitenberg and Richard Dean Burns. Santa Barbara, Calif.: ABC-Clio, 1973.

A brief chronology and a detailed bibliography of the U.S. involvement in Vietnam. The major issues of the war are also delineated.

World Hunger: A Guide to the Economic and Political Dimensions. Nicole Ball. Santa Barbara, Calif.: ABC-Clio, 1981.

Hunger is not simply a technological problem. Its remedy entails economic and political change. The author provides the most complete bibliography on the topic of hunger. The book offers a complete index, and each topical subsection is preceded by an introduction. It also includes a glossary of terms but the bibliography is not annotated.

2e BOOK REVIEWS

Book reviews are published in scholarly periodicals and in newspapers. They are an especially important secondary source and play a legitimate role in research. But book reviews are at best a supplement to, not a substitute for, reading the original manuscript. Read a book review before reading the book and you will find it easier to pick out the main points; read the review after reading the book and you have a laboratory check on the difference between your thinking and the reviewer's. Do not hesitate to cite the opinions of reviewers when dealing with a book on which the paper is relying.

Book Review Digest. New York: H. W. Wilson, 1905—.

A monthly publication, this is an indexed reference to selected book reviews drawn from about 75 English and American periodicals. With its emphasis on popular rather than scholarly journals, it is arranged by author and has title and subject indexes. Each issue covers from 300 to 400 titles. Excerpts from several reviews are presented for each book, along with a bibliography. For reviews of more scholarly books see *Social Sciences Citation.*

Book Review Index. Detroit: Gale Research, Co. 1965—.

To a great extent this monthly review, with quarterly and annual cumulations, supplements the *Book Review Digest.* The index lists current book reviews in the social and natural sciences, although no excerpts of reviews are given, and there is an author index only.

Perspective: Monthly Review of New Books in Government, Politics and International Affairs. Washington, D.C.: Helen Dwight Reed Educational Foundation, 1972—.

Formerly published in Washington, D.C., by Heldef Publications. Each monthly issue contains concise reviews broken down by the subfields in political science. The reviews are written by specialists in each subfield, and they are signed. Unlike reviews in a general periodical, these emphasize the specialized issues involved in each subfield; i.e., a review of a book on the presidency emphasizes how the book fits into the various political science theories regarding presidential power.

The Political Science Reviewer. Hampden-Sydney, Va.: The Political Science Reviewer, 1971—.
  Formerly titled and listed under *The Political Science Reviewer: An Annual Review of Books.* Bryn Mawr, Pa.: Intercollegiate's Studies Institute, 1971—.
  Although presented as a series of book reviews, this source contains lengthy philosophical essays going well beyond the boundaries of usual book reviews. Fewer than 10 books are reviewed per issue, each review useful as an idea piece.

2f INDEXES TO PERIODICIALS, BOOKS, AND DOCUMENTS

An index is a detailed list of names, terms, subjects, places, or other significant items in a complete work with exact page or references to the material itself. It is the standard bridge to library material. Included in the following indexes are:

1. Standard periodical indexes which cover a broad group of periodicals in all subjects, *e.g.*, the *Reader's Guide* for popular periodicals, the *Social Sciences Index* for academic periodicals.

2. Special source indexes which focus on a special kind of source of material, *e.g.*, the *Alternative Press Index*, or a single source such as *Wall Street Journal Index*.

3. Special subject indexes which concentrate on a special subject in a variety of sources, periodicals, books, and documents. Example: *The Environment Index*.

Indexes obviously can save much time in finding appropriate material. They are also a good source of ideas. For example, if one knows he or she is generally interested in a topic such as recent U.S. politics but needs help in narrowing the topic, indexes such as the *Social Sciences Index* may be used to identify a number of well-defined areas for exploration, in this case executive power, corruption in politics, lobbyists, political participation, and others, would be found.

ABC POL SCI A Bibliography of Contents: Political Science & Government. Santa Barbara, Calif.: American Bibliographical Center. Clio Press, 1969—.
  A guide to about 300 periodicals in political science and government as well as related disciplines. Articles are indexed by journal, subject, and author. *ABC POL SCI* is published five times a year with annual and five-year indexes.

American Statistics Index. Washington, D.C.: Congressional Information Service, 1972—.

A useful master guide and index to all statistical publications released by the U.S. government. This publication both indexes and abstracts statistical publications.

Alternative Press Index. Toronto, Canada: Alternative Press Center, 1969—.

A host of important current issues are covered quite differently in nontraditional, rather than in traditional newspapers. These include gay liberation, antiwar efforts, alternative lifestyles, etc. This source indexes by subject 188 alternative newspapers, lists them by complete name and tells where they can be obtained.

Asian Recorder. New Delhi: Asian Recorder, 1955—.

(Annotated in Chapter 3e.)

Anthologies By and About Women: An Analytical Index. Susan Cardinale. Westport, Conn.: Greenwood Press, 1982.

As a subject for study, women in society and politics has become a matter of central concern for serious students of society. The literature in this field is well organized with this valuable index.

Biography Index. New York: H. W. Wilson, 1947—.

This quarterly with cumulations is the key index to biographical material. It includes all the biographical references. Entries are arranged alphabetically with a subject index in the back of each issue. The subject index is especially helpful in identifying important individuals in a particular field who are receiving public attention.

Congressional Information Service Index to Publications of the United States Congress. Washington, D.C., 1970—.

(Annotated in Chapter 4d.)

Constitutions of the United States, National and State Index. Legislative Drafting Service Research Fund, Columbia University. Dobbs Ferry, N.Y.: Oceana, 1962—.

(Annotated in Chapter 4e.)

Canadian News Facts: The Indexed Digest of Canadian Current Events. Barrie Martland and Stephen D. Pepper, eds. Toronto, Ont.: Marpep, 1967—.

(Annotated in Chapter 3e.)

CBS News Index. New York: Microfilming Corporation of America, 1975.

This thorough index of all CBS news broadcasts has been available in hardcover editions since 1975. The broadcast transcripts are available on 35mm microfilm or microfiche. Separate hardcover editions of the broadcast *Face The Nation* are also available. With this material, original research comparing quality, depth, bias, etc. of news coverage may be conducted.

Cumulative Book Index. New York: H. W. Wilson, 1898—.

This monthly index with cumulations provides a comprehensive list of all new books published in various areas of interest, some of which might not be found in a college library, and usually lists the other works by each author published within the time span covered. Also of value to the researcher is a selected list of important government documents included in the index. Since 1925 the *Cumulative Book Index* has included books in the English language that are published outside the United States. Books are listed by author, title, and subject.

Cumulative Index to the Proceedings of the American Political Science Association. Washington, D.C.: American Political Science Association, 1904–1912, 1956–1969. Compiled by Mark Iris. Ann Arbor, Mich.: University Microfilms, 1970.

The American Political Science Association is the main professional organization in the United States for political scientists. This index lists scholarly papers presented at its meetings during the given years. It is useful to illustrate how research in a particular area is progressing.

Decennial Cumulative Index 1941-1950. 2 vols. Washington, D.C.: Government Printing Office, 1953; reprinted, Detroit: Gale Research Company, 1971—.

Supplemented by an index series published yearly, *Numerical Lists and Schedules of Volumes of the Reports and Documents,* for each session of Congress.

Education Index. New York: H. W. Wilson, 1929—.

This reference, published monthly except for July and August, with compilations, is a subject index to educational periodicals, yearbooks, and bulletins as well as to the publications of the United States Office of Education since 1929. It indexes the answers to such questions as: What is the latest method of educating the mentally handicapped? How much money is being spent by the national government on education?

Energy Index: A Select Guide to Energy Information Since 1970. New York: Environment Information Center, 1973—.

A massive collection of information on the energy problem, laws, citations, companies, and energy resources. Although much of the work is technical, simply glancing through it suggests many fresh avenues of exploration with regard to this crucial problem.

The Environment Index: A Guide to the Key Environmental Literature of the Year. New York: Environment Information Center, 1971—.

Reviews major developments, including a summary, of key legislation, important patents, and citations to books and films on the environment. Much of the work is highly technical, but the book offers the social science researcher specialized references in a convenient form.

Essay and General Literature Index. New York: H. W. Wilson, 1900—.

Published semiannually with accumulations and supplements, it specifically catalogs the contents of books rather than periodicals—which is helpful because often essays and articles appear in a book of collected works without being specifically referred to in the title of the book. This index can help locate, for example, an article on "Woodrow Wilson and Southern Congressmen" that appeared in a book edited by Sidney Fine, titled *Recent America* (New York: Crowell-Collier and Macmillan, 1962).

Guide to U.S. Government Statistics. 4th ed. John L. Andriot. McLean, Va.: Documents Index, 1973—.

(Annotated in Chapter 4a.)

Index to the Christian Science Monitor. Boston: Christian Science Monitor, 1960—.

Published monthly with semiannual and annual cumulations.

Index to Current Urban Documents. Westport, Conn.: Greenwood Periodicals, 1972—.

This is the only guide to reports on urban problems issued by the larger cities and counties in the United States and Canada. For example, if a person is interested in manpower training programs, one can find references to reports from major cities. It is useful if one is looking for first-hand resources.

Index to Legal Periodicals. American Associations of Law Libraries. New York: H. W. Wilson, 1909—.

Law journals interpret the law; they are also an excellent source of public policy articles on such topics as the regulation of business. This index contains data on about 300 journals and is published monthly with annual cumulations.

Index to International Public Opinion, 1978-79—. Elizabeth Hann Hastings and Philip K. Hastings. Westport, Conn.: Greenwood Press, 1979.

(Annotated in Chapter 4a.)

Index to the Times. John Gurnett, ed. Reading, England: Newspaper Archive Developments, 1906—.

Since 1972 it has been published under the title, *The Times Index.*

Index to U.S. Government Periodicals. Chicago: Infordata International Incorporated, 1975—.

Provides access to every periodical published by the U.S. government in which substantive articles are printed. Thus, more than 100 agencies of the U.S. government publish periodicals such as *Army Lawyer* and the *Journal of the National Cancer Institute.* This publication indexes 175 selected titles by author and subject and the articles often contain little cited but valuable sources.

International Bibliography of Political Science. 9 vols. The International Committee for Social Sciences Documentation. Chicago: Aldine, 1952-76; Paris: UNESCO, Vol. 9; London: Tavlstock Publications, 1977—.
   (Annotated in Chapter 2d.)

New York Times Index. New York: New York Times, 1851-1906 and 1912—.
   The major reference source for an accurate chronological list of important events. Published semimonthly with annual cumulations since 1930, this publication presents an extensive and detailed look at the world news as reported by the *New York Times.* It cites the date, page, and column, with many cross references and serves as a reference for material in other newspapers as well. One of the features that students find most attractive is the brief synopsis under each entry, which frequently makes reference to the newspaper itself unnecessary.

New York Times Obituaries Index 1858-1968. New York: New York Times, 1970.
   The obituaries of the *New York Times* are far more thorough than those of most newspapers. They are often the most complete biographical information available. This source helps find this information.

Poole's Index to Periodical Literature. rev. ed. Gloucester, Mass.: Peter Smith, 1938.
   Although not as comprehensive as the *Readers' Guide to Periodical Literature,* this is still the best index of nineteenth-century periodicals. It includes poems and stories and covers approximately 1800-1906. It can be used to research such subjects as the political attitudes expressed in American periodicals of that time.

Public Affairs Information Service Bulletin. Robert S. Wilson, ed. New York: Public Affairs Information Service, 1915—.
   This index, with annual cumulations, unifies a wide variety of sources concerned with public affairs. Besides periodicals, it lists books, pamphlets, and government documents. The subjects include economics, social conditions, politics, and international relations. Most entries also include brief explanations of the item.

Readers' Guide to Periodical Literature. New York: H. W. Wilson, 1901—.
   The major periodical reference source that lists author and subject in a single index and covers the most popular, nontechnical periodicals in the English language.

Social Sciences Citation Index. Philadelphia, Pa.: Institute for Scientific Information, 1973.

Indexes over 1,000 social science periodicals in three new ways.
1) a citation index allows one to trace the application of an idea by showing how and where a particular author is cited within a calendar year;
2) a source index that, besides containing the usual bibliographic information, lists every citation in a particular article;
3) there is "permuterm," in which every significant word in the title is matched with the author of that article.

Social Sciences Index. New York: H. W. Wilson, 1916—.

This index, which has quarterly compilations, provides the best source for developing an academic and theoretical focus for a term paper. For example, under general headings such as "interest groups," there are scholarly articles outlining the pros and cons of the various political science approaches to the study of interest groups. These articles provide a useful frame of reference for the study of a particular group. In June 1965 the name of this reference was changed from *International Index* to *Social Science and Humanities Index.* More recently a separate *Humanities Index* has been published. Book reviews are now indexed separately at the end of each volume.

Television News Index and Abstracts. Vanderbilt Television News Archive, Joint University Libraries. Nashville, Tenn. 1968—.

A monthly publication that indexes the evening newscasts of the three major commercial television networks, ABC, CBS, NBC. The index begins August 5, 1968.

UNDOC CURRENT INDEX. New York: United Nations, 1950—.

The UN documentation system is shockingly cryptographic and is impossible to penetrate without this key, published monthly. A general description of the documents is found in *A Guide to the Use of United Nations Documents.* But this index must be used if one is to keep abreast of or locate specific documents. Prior to 1979 this source was called UNDEX, and printed in three parts: Series A, Subjects; Series B, Countries; Series C, List of Documents. These three sections are now contained in one volume.

United States Political Science Documents (USPSD). Pittsburgh: University of Pittsburgh Press, 1975—.

A selective but thorough service, this publication concentrates on indexing and abstracting articles in what are considered important or leading journals. Each annual edition contains two parts. Part 1 indexes articles by author, subject, journal, and other methods. Part 2 contains the abstracted article, persons cited in each article, key subjects, and proper names. This is a carefully executed and very useful project.

The Wall Street Journal Index. New York: M. Dow Jones, 1955—.

An excellent source for studying powerful economic figures and the relationship between government and the economic elites.

World Treaty Index. (Preliminary 2d ed.) Peter Roh, ed. Seattle: Treaty Research Center, University of Washington, 1981.

This index serves as far more than a simple locater of treaties. It applies the techniques of modern quantitative research to the ancient field of international law. It can be used as a basis for original research. The multitude of treaties signed by nations of the world have been content-analyzed and indexed in depth. For example, if one wishes to compare how nations protect their citizens when abroad, one would look up "protection of nationals" and find citations to 17 specific treaties dealing with this problem.

3

Summaries and Shortened Versions of Information

Authors and readers do not always have the same goals. Authors often want to present all they know about a particular topic such as the 1984 Democratic Presidential Primaries. This might be much more than the reader might wish or need to know of Gary Hart's Campaign in New Hampshire. In such instances it is extremely useful to have a summary of basic information. This chapter contains a number of such shortened versions of politically significant bodies of information. Encyclopedias are general covering basic information on a wide range of topics. Other types of sources are much narrower. The focus might be upon a specialized subject area such as the activities of the United Nations. In other instances the emphasis might be on a particular type of information, such as the summaries of yearly events in almanacs and yearbooks. This chapter breaks these sources down into several major divisions: encyclopedias, dictionaries and glossaries, almanacs, atlases and yearbooks, biographic material, handbooks, directories and guides. It also discusses how to use this information.

HANDBOOKS, DIRECTORIES, AND GUIDES

Handbooks, directories and guides are defined as concise summaries of a body of information. In these sources you will find the key ideas and the important boundaries surrounding a particular body of study. These works can be used as basic sources for research, as a bridge to other sources, or as a source of ideas for defining a topic.

Handbooks, directories, and guides have been divided into seven basic groups:

Discipline and Subfield
Information Sources
Political Activism
Politically Significant Groups and Organizations

Regions and Countries of the World
Political Events, Historic
Political Events, Current

3a Discipline and Subfield Handbooks and Guides

Textbooks in political science and in its various subfields usually contain introductory discussions of the scope and methods of the discipline. Because of space limitations, however, these textbooks rarely provide in-depth information and summaries helpful in organizing the body of literature in a given field. The entries annotated below may be used to aid in filling that gap.

Dictionary of the History of Ideas. New York: Charles Scribner and Sons, 1973.
(Annotated in Chapter 3j.)

Encyclopedia of American Foreign Policy. 3 vols. New York: Charles Scribner and Sons, 1978.
(Annotated in Chapter 3k.)

The Future of the Future. John McHale. New York: George Braziller, 1969.
Examines the context, issues, methodology, and problems of studying the future. It is readable and useful for the study of a variety of current political problems.

Guide to Public Administration. D. A. Cutchin. Itasca, Ill.: F. E. Peacock Publishers, Inc., 1981.
Contains a useful glossary of concepts, theories, names, and statutes, and a fine annotated bibliography of research sources in public administration.

Handbook of Research Design and Social Measurement. 3rd ed. Delbert C. Miller. New York: David McKay Company, Inc., 1977.
(Annotated in Chapter 4b.)

The Handbook of Political Behavior. Samuel Long, ed. New York: Plenum, 1981.
This five-volume set brings together current thinking in the fields of political psychology and political sociology. Contains 20 contributions by subject specialists on such topics as small-group behavior, political socialization, political violence, and judicial behavior.

Handbook of Political Psychology. Jeanne N. Knutson. San Francisco: Jossey Bass, 1973.
What influences political behavior? Most psychologists agree that the list of factors would include those items that influence all behavior. These sophis-

ticated essays illustrate the interface between psychology and politics, i.e., personality, political attitudes, socialization, the authoritarian personality, patterns of leadership, aggression, revolution, and war.

Handbook of Political Science. 8 vols. Fred I. Greenstein and Nelson W. Polsby, eds. Reading, Mass.: Addison-Wesley Publishing Company, 1975.

Particularly useful for advanced students, the *Handbook* is a collection of essays on a number of analytically relevant topics within the field of political science. Topics include, "The Logic of Political Inquiry: A Synthesis of Opposed Perspectives;" "Political Development;" and "Interest Groups." Essays are written by subject specialists and provide a good understanding of the state of the art.

Human Behavior: An Inventory of Scientific Findings. Bernard Berelson and Gary Steiner. New York: Harcourt Brace Jovanovich, 1964.

Inventory is the key word in this title. An easy-to-read inventory of hundreds of propositions about human behavior, many of which can be related to political behavior. Each research finding is concisely explored and illustrated. Examples of findings: People with well-adjusted personalities are more likely to be active politically; class is more important in determining political views in urban than in rural areas.

Latin American Research Review: A Journal for the Communication of Research Among Individuals and Institutions Concerned with Studies in Latin America. Editorial Office. Austin, Texas: University of Texas, 1965—.

The basic guide to research in Latin American studies, this book is usually divided into parts: "Topic Reviews," four or more pieces outlining research on subjects from literature to taxes; "Reports," which follows the latest trends in research and sources; "Current Research Inventory"—the soul of the entire journal—which lists by university and subject all post-doctoral research reported; "Forum," a discussion of current questions in the area. The journal has been called "an absolute must for any library where there is the slightest interest in Latin American affairs." We agree.

Masterpieces of World Philosophy in Summary Form. Frank N. Magill, ed. New York: Harper & Row, 1963.

Some academicians feel that students of philosophy or political theory must gain their understanding from the original works of the philosophers themselves with little or no outside assistance. There is room for disagreement. Although it is always beneficial to read the original, most students can help sharpen their understanding by outside direction. A glance at one of the summaries offered is likely to raise the student's level of comprehension. Also, there are times when it is neither wise nor possible to read an entire work, in which case this reference can save the day.

Primer on Constitutional Law. Albert P. Melone and Carl Kalvelage. Pacific Palisades, Calif.: Palisades Publishers, 1982.
(Annotated in Chapter 2d.)

Public Adminstration Moves Into the Eighties: A Bibliography and Survey of the Field. Howard E. McCurdy. 2d ed., New York: Marcel-Dekker, 1984.
(Annotated in Chapter 2d.)

Research Essentials of Administrative Law. H. B. Jacobini, Albert P. Melone, Carl Kalvelage. Pacific Palisades, Calif.: Palisades Publishers, 1983.
This book guides students of administrative law to the research materials and other sources for studying the topic.

Sources of Democracy: Voices of Freedom, Hope, and Justice. Saul K. Padover. New York: McGraw-Hill, 1973.
Contains ideas, documents, and statements about democracy with special applied sections on current problem areas such as justice and race relations. It is a good first stop for an idea paper.

3b Information Sources

Sources of information form a never-ending chain. Each source, such as this book, is also a bridge to more specialized sources. In this section are both general information sources similar to this one and other more specialized works.

Directory of Archives and Manuscript Repositories. National Historical Publications and Records Commission. Washington, D.C.: National Archives and Records Service, General Service Administration, 1978.
A guide to all archives and manuscript repositories in the United States and its territories. Contains names, addresses, telephone numbers, and holdings descriptions of each of the 2,676 centers. Organized alphabetically by states, it also contains a good subject index. This can be a useful source for researchers interested in locating difficult-to-obtain historical manuscripts.

Confidential Information Sources: Public and Private. John Carroll. Los Angeles: Security World, 1975.
John Carroll has spent a lifetime as a private investigator. This book is a guide to the *legal* use of a wide variety of information sources including motor vehicle records, the Internal Revenue Service, the Census Bureau, etc.

Directory of Information Resources in the United States. The National Referral Center for Science and Technology of the Library of Congress. Washington, D.C.: Government Printing Office, published irregularly.
(Annotated in Chapter 4c.)

Freedom of Information Guide: Citizens' Guide to the Use of the Freedom of Information and Privacy Acts. Washington, D.C.: WANT Publishing Company, 1982.

This publication tells how to request information from the national government.

Guide to Reference Books. 9th ed. Eugene Paul Sheehy. Chicago: American Library Association, 1976.

The most comprehensive of all guides of this type, it was first published in 1902 and through nine editions and supplements has remained conspicuously up-to-date. The latest edition divides 7,500 titles into five categories: general reference works; humanities, social sciences; history and area studies; and the pure and applied sciences.

Guide to the Study of International Relations. J. K. Zawodny. San Francisco: Chandler, 1966.

This guide is a paperback volume designed to find the widely scattered and often complex materials tied to the study of international relations/ government documents, national archives materials, UN publications, and up-to-date, empirically validated findings in the behavioral sciences. It holds more than 500 cross-indexed entries classified under subject headings that, except for the journals, have been annotated and can guide one efficiently through several million titles to the specific one desired.

A Guide to Library Sources in Political Science: American Government. Clement E. Vose. Washington, D.C.: American Political Science Association, 1975.

This is the first in a series of specialized monographs on library sources. It is unusual in that it is truly a work of original scholarship about library sources. Various sources such as dictionaries and encyclopedias are compared and analyzed with reference to individual items.

A Bibliographic Guide to Educational Research. Dorthea M. Berry. Second edition. The Scarecrow Press, Inc. Metuchen, New Jersey, 1980.

Although it is directed to the education major, this handbook's basic instruction in the use of the library should benefit all students. It describes all of the reference sources listed in this guide, including a number of highly specialized guides to colleges and universities.

International and Regional Politics in the Middle East and North Africa: A Guide to Information Sources. Ann Schulz. Detroit, Mich.: Gale Research Co., 1977.

This is volume 6 in the International Relations Information Guide Series published by the Gale Research Company. In this volume, subjects are divided into eight chapters containing annotations for the following areas: resource materials for Middle East politics, regional issues, foreign policies of Middle Eastern states divided by each state in the region, external powers in the region, the Arab-Israeli conflict, petroleum, reference works, and serials.

International Organizations: A Guide to Information Sources. Alexine Atherton. Detroit: Gale Research, 1976.

Fully annotated with highly detailed topical organization, current and historical. Includes all the social and technical units of the United Nations, political implications of international organizations, peacekeeping, etc.

A Reader's Guide to the Social Sciences. Bert F. Hoselitz, ed. rev. ed. Glencoe, Ill.: The Free Press, 1970.

Divides into sections on history, geography, sociology, anthropology, psychology, economics, and political science. The last chapter is written by Heinz Eulau; it is a splendid introduction to the more important studies in political science.

Research Centers Directory. 8th ed. Archie M. Palmer, ed. Detroit: Gale Research, 1983 (supplemented).

Much research conducted in the United States is carried out by university related and independently operated think-tanks. This directory contains more than 6,000 entries listing the names, addresses, phone numbers, and descriptions of research centers relating to all aspects of science, social science, government, law, and other relevant fields. Students may wish to write or call these centers for publications or other useful information.

Social Science Reference Sources: A Practical Guide. Tze-Chung Li. Westport, Conn. Greenwood Press, 1980.

A reference book on sources in all the social sciences, broadly defined. Chapter 16 contains information on political science guides. bibliographies, indexes, and abstracts, dictionaries, biographies, directories, yearbooks, handbooks, and periodicals. Yet because political science is highly interdisciplinary, sources for the other social sciences should be consulted from time to time. This book will point to these sources.

Information Sources of Political Science. 3rd ed. Frederick L. Holler. Santa Barbara, Calif.: ABC-Clio, 1981.

(Annotated in Chapter 2d.)

Sources of Information in the Social Sciences: A Guide to Literature. ed. Carl M. White et al. Chicago: American Library Association, 1973.

Besides general reference works, this source offers separate treatments for history, economics and business administration, sociology, anthropology, psychology, education, and political science. Each chapter is complete with introduction, important studies, bibliographies, and data sources. The volume is geared for the interdisciplinary and behavioral approach to the social sciences.

Washington Information Directory 1982-83. Washington, D.C. Congressional Quarterly, Inc., 1982—.
     This annual publication is a comprehensive guide to U.S. government and private information sources by subject. Contains detailed subject/agency and organization index and provides the names, telephone numbers, addresses, and responsibilities of information sources.

The World of Learning. London: Europa, 1947—.
     Contains basic descriptions, and a list of responsible individuals in a worldwide directory of colleges, universities, research institutes, museums, libraries, and archives is also included. It has a first-rate index that allows one to identify all the organizations involved in each area of interest.

3c Political Activism

     Political science can also be a guide to action, a participatory rather than a purely spectator sport. To this end, these sources are helpful.

     The American Civil Liberties Union publishes a series of handbooks that explain legal rights in plain language. Each handbook describes the rights of a particular group: voters, union members, teachers, students, veterans, reporters, hospitals, patients, and others. Examples from the series follow.
E. Carrington Boggan. *The Rights of Gay People: The ACLU Guide to a Gay Person's Rights.* New York: Discus Books, 1975.
Richard E. Blumbery. *The Rights of Tenants: The Basic ACLU Guide to a Tenant's Rights.* New York: Avon, 1978.
Richard E. Larsen. *The Rights of Racial Minorities.* New York: Avon Books, 1980 (or ACLU Books).
Susan Ross. *The Rights of Women: The Basic ACLU Guide to a Women's Rights.* Sunrise Books, 1973.
Alan Sussman. *The Rights of Young People: The Basic ACLU Guide to a Young Person's Rights.* New York: Avon Books, 1977.

Access to Federal Agencies. James R. Michael, ed. Ralph Nader's Center for the Study of Responsive Law. New York: Basic Books, 1974.
     Political scientists have spent much more time studying the inner workings of the Congress than they have of the bureaucracy. The action-oriented Nader groups have more than made up for this. This source pulls together much of the work of Ralph Nader and his various groups for the past 10 years. Although written in journalistic style, it contains a great deal of basic information available nowhere else. The main thrusts are how bureaucratic agencies operate; how to get information about and from them, both officially and unofficially;

how they use administrative procedure; and how a researcher can use it. There is also a long chapter on individual agencies.

Capitol Hill Manual. Frank Cummings. Washington, D.C.: The Bureau of National Affairs, Inc., 1976.

This is a "how to" book. Besides members of Congress, lobbyists, and the press, students interested in learning the nuts and bolts of law-making in Washington, D.C. will find this manual valuable.

Election Campaign Handbook. Daniel Gaby and Merle Treusch. Englewood Cliffs, N.J.: Prentice-Hall, 1976.

A loose-leaf, very practical, how-to-do-it guide. Emphasizes the actual steps to take in signing up volunteers, how to write fund raising letters, how to set up a get-out-the-vote campaign, etc.

Encyclopedia of U.S. Government Benefits. Roy A. Grisham, Jr., and Paul D. McConaughy, eds. New York: Everest House, 1981.

Lists, describes, and discusses all services and benefits provided by the United States government. It provides answers to the complex question of the citizen's relationship to big government. This is the first book to catalog and detail eligibility for all government services. It is also unique because it alphabetizes primarily by benefit classification rather than by agency, department, or initiating legislative act. It is both a practical reference and a useful index to the scope and depth of federal programs.

The Compact Guide to Parliamentary Procedure. Harvey Cromwell. New York: Crowell, 1973.

While *Roberts Rules of Order* remains the basic source in this field, this handy guide provides quick, on-the-spot information on how to put questions on the floor, amend motions, reconsider, etc.

Grass Roots: An Anti-Nuke Source Book. Fred Wilcox, ed. Trumansbery, N.Y.: The Crossing Press, 1980.

A how-to-do-it book for the anti-nuclear activist. Articles on a wide variety of direct action tactics, non-violence theory, how to detect low level radiation, refuting arguments for nuclear power, challenging local utility companies, etc. While the articles are specifically aimed at the anti-nuclear area, many of the direct action techniques such as peaceful demonstration would be applicable to a number of other areas.

How to Get Things Changed: A Handbook for Tackling Community Problems. Bert Strauss and Mary E. Stowe. Garden City, N.Y.: Doubleday, 1974.

The authors base their experience on a federally sponsored community-change project in Virginia. The special values of the book are the concrete suggestions for accomplishing the nitty-gritty aspects of community change, i.e., the idea of using a facilitator rather than a chairperson for a meeting, strategies of organization, etc. The book can also be useful for an academic research paper as a framework or criterion for examining other change efforts.

How Federal Laws Are Made: Citizen's Guide to the Federal Lawmaking Process, from Introduction of a Bill, to Enactment, to Issuance of Agency Regulations. Washington, D.C.: WANT Publishing Company, 1982.

A practical approach to law-making, this easy-to-use reference contains a guide on how to use the *Federal Register* and the *Code of Federal Regulations.*

Playing to Win. Jeff Greenfield. Simon & Schuster, New York, 1980.

Less a concrete how-to-do-it book than an incisive and somewhat cynical view of how hard the game of politics is currently being played. Covers the important campaign areas such as "how to give a speech" and "how to use the press," with numerous current examples from U.S. national scenes.

The Population Activist's Handbook. The Population Institute. New York: Macmillan, 1974.

Theorizing about population control is one thing, doing something about it is another. The first section in this source focuses on action; dealing with policy, political tactics, how to work with officeholders, etc. The second section deals with the use of research as an action tactic and tells how to conduct polls, surveys, etc. as a step toward awareness and resolution of the population problem. Section three deals with actual change tactics such as how to set up services related to abortion, VD, etc. The worldwide implications of the population problem are discussed in the last section.

Robert's Rules of Order Newly Revised. Henry M. Robert. Revised by Sarah Corbin Robert. Homewood, Ill.: Scott, Foresman and Co., 1981.

Shaped and strengthened by U.S. courts since it first appeared in 1876, this authority is widely accepted as the last word in parliamentary procedure. It is the sine qua non to understanding the goals, motivations, methods, and priorities of most formally organized assemblies in the world.

3d Political Groups and Organizations

These sources guide one to the players in the political game. If one is intrigued by a particular policy area or event but is not sure how to investigate it, a good first step is to learn about the key political groups and organizations in the area.

A Is A: Libertarian Directory. Dale Haviland. Brighton, Mich.: Mega, 1972.

Libertarianism is a growing political movement in the United States. Although it includes many cleavages and points of view, its proponents generally support individual rights, personal liberty, and laissez-faire capitalism. This is both a philosophical explanation of libertarianism and a practical guide to other sources, individuals, and organizations dedicated to libertarian principles.

American Agencies Interested in International Affairs. 5th ed. Donald Wasson, ed. The Council on Foreign Relations. New York: Praeger, 1964—.

Guide to several hundred organizations based in the United States, it covers their purpose and organizational structure.

American Politics Yearbook 1982-83. Jarol B. Manheim. New York: Longman, Inc., 1982.

A guide to government agencies, interest groups, political parties, lobbyists, bureaucrats, members of Congress, the executive and judicial branches, and policy think-tanks. Contains names, addresses, and descriptions in one paragraph each.

Civil Rights Directory, 1981. U.S. Commission on Civil Rights. Clearinghouse Publication 15 (revised), 1981.

Lists the hundreds of government agencies and private groups which are involved with the enforcement, administration, and monitoring of federal and state equal opportunity laws. Provides descriptions, addresses, and telephone numbers for each public or private organization.

Encyclopedia of Associations. 18th ed. Denise S. Akey, ed. Detroit: Gale Research, 1983.

(Annotated in Chapter 3k.)

Encyclopedia of Governmental Advisory Organizations. 3rd ed. Linda E. Sullivan, ed. Detroit, Michigan: Gale Research Co., 1980.

(Annotated in Chapter 3k.)

Environment U.S.A.: A Guide to Agencies, People, and Resources. The Onyx Group, Inc., ed., Glenn L. Paulson, adv. ed. New York: R. R. Bowker, 1974.

The ecological revolution has spawned a whole host of groups and programs. This work contains useful essays on the laws and policies and an exhaustive directory of the participants in environmental policy.

European Institutions: Co-operation, Integration, Unification. 3rd ed. Arthur H. Robertson. New York: Matthew Bender, 1973.

A complete guide to the many organizations now involved in European integration. It includes political, economic, and social organizations. The essays are both factual and interpretative.

Everyman's United Nations. 9th ed. New York: United Nations Department of Public Information, 1979—.

(Annotated in Chapter 4c.)

Federal Regulatory Directory 1981-82. Washington, D.C., Congressional Quarterly, Inc., 1981—.

Published biennially, this directory outlines the organization, functions, and enforcement authority of 13 federal regulatory agencies. Also, it provides descriptions of some other agencies. Lists staff, names, addresses, and telephone numbers of the agencies' central, regional, and area offices.

First National Directory of "Rightist" Groups: Publications and Some Individuals. 6th ed. Los Angeles: Alert Americans Association, 1968.

The Who's Who of the political right from the National Fluoridation News to four Reagan-for-President centers. This book is, however, only a directory of names and addresses and contains no description of entries.

Human Rights Organizations and Periodicals Directory 1979-1980. David Christiano, ed. Berkeley, Calif. Meiklejohn Civil Liberties Institute, 1979.

This directory is an excellent guide to sources of information on human rights. Contains names, addresses, phone numbers, and discussion of U.S. based human rights organizations. Also contains similar information on periodicals concerned with human rights. Further editions are anticipated.

International Organizations: A Guide to Information Sources. Alexine L. Atherton, ed. Detroit: Gale Research, 1976.

(Annotated in Chapter 3b.)

Key Influences in the American Right. Ferdinand V. Solara. Washington, D.C.: LEA Communications, 1974.

Published in 1972 by Polifax of Denver. This new volume is completely revised and reorganized. In addition to a brief description, one finds in this volume the addresses, officers, membership, etc., of American rightist groups. This source contains an introductory essay and typology of rightist groups and ideas, which can serve as a useful framework for a paper.

The National Directory of State Agencies 1980-1981. Nancy D. Wright and Gene P. Allen. Herner and Company, Compilers, Arlington, Va.: Information Resources Press, 1980.

This is the fourth biennial edition. It contains: alphabetical listing of state agency functions, ranging from adjutant general to workers' compensation; state government telephone information numbers and addresses; state agencies listed alphabetically by state; state agencies by functions; and an appendix which lists the names, addresses, and phone numbers of associations of state government officials. Researchers on a given topic can write and call appropriate agencies for information. Often, although not necessarily, state agency officials are pleased to aid students in research projects, especially if the topic is of concern to them. The student should explain that he or she will provide the agency with a copy of the paper in return for its cooperation.

National Trade and Professional Associations of the United States and Canada, and Labor Unions. Craig Colgate, Jr., ed. Washington, D.C.: Columbia, annual.

If anyone had doubts about the importance of business groups in American politics, the experience of Watergate certainly should have dispelled that belief. Here are all the players in the game of influencing public policy. Most helpful are key words where are listed all groups involved in particular areas as well as indexes of budgets from $10,000 (the Socket Screw Products Bureau) to over $1 million (Asphalt Institute) and of key executives.

Political Handbook of the World: 1981. Arthur S. Banks and William Overstreet, eds. New York: McGraw Hill Book Co., 1981.

This edition is the successor to various political handbooks published in cooperation with the Council on Foreign Relations. It is a global compendium of governments, regional issues, and international organizations. Contains discussions on the significant world and regional issues for the 1980 calendar year. Future volumes are anticipated.

Political Parties and Civic Action Groups. Edward L. Schapsmeier and Frederick H. Schapsmeier. Westport, Conn.: Greenwood Press, 1981.

A handy one-volume encyclopedia of organized groups, past and present, which are involved in the U.S. political process.

The PAC Directory: A Complete Guide to Political Action Committees. Edited by Marvin Weinberg. Cambridge, Mass.: Ballinger Publishing Co., 1982.

The Federal Elections Campaign Act of 1974 limited the amount an individual may contribute to a federal candidate, but this same legislation opened the door to contributions of a committee made from business or labor. The result is the growing importance of political action committees in the American politics. This source provides a listing of each committee, its receipts and contributions and a detailed listing of the contributions made to candidates.

Political Parties in Europe. Theo Stammen. Translated by Gunda Cannon-Kern. London: John Martin Publishing Ltd., 1980.

More than a reference work, this translated volume contains considerable information on Western European political parties. About half the book is devoted to the parties; the remainder is a discussion and analysis, with documents, of the movement toward European political integration.

Washington V: A Comprehensive Directory of the Nation's Capital People and Institutions. Cary Grayson, Jr. and Susan Lukowski, eds. Washington, D.C.: Potomac, 1979.

This excellent one-stop guide to the nation's capital includes international, national, state, and local agencies headquartered in the District of Columbia. It also lists embassies, private and nonprofit organizations such as American Civil Liberties Union, press, TV, radio, private clubs, lawyers associations, labor unions, research associations, foundations, and numerous community groups. This book can save a visitor to Washington much valuable time and lead to the right organization to answer questions.

World Communism: A Handbook 1918-1965. Witold S. Sworakowski, ed. Stanford, Calif.: Hoover Institution Press, 1973.

The Communist Party has been active in 116 countries during this period. This source contains a brief essay on its activities in each of those countries. The book is a good first source for a variety of topics focusing on the history, organization, techniques of party operation, etc.

3e Regions and Countries of the World

Many American sources such as the *Reader's Guide* have only a limited focus on other regions and countries of the world. These sources draw together a variety of information sources around key areas of the world.

Africa Diary. New Delhi: Africa Publications, 1961—.

A weekly diary of African events, with an index. Although the summaries are brief, they are probably more extensive than one finds in a United States paper. This book provides a good way to follow an event without endlessly thumbing through newspapers. Sources for each entry are listed. There are quarterly and annual cumulations.

Africa: A Handbook to the Continent. rev. ed. Colin Legum, ed. New York: Praeger, 1966.

Deals with individual African countries, the continent as a whole, and other countries' attitudes toward Africa.

African Encyclopedia. London: Oxford University Press, 1974.

This is a good one-volume source on Africa. In addition to listing a number of African topics not available elsewhere, it provides a detailed index of African subjects and indicates how to deal with them.

African Recorder. New Delhi: Recorder Press, 1962—.

This publication summarizes events and quotes in African affairs twice monthly from major worldwide newspapers.

Arab Report and Record. London: Arab Report and Record, 1966—. Published twice monthly, this work has the usual news summaries plus related statistics such as weekly Arab oil production figures.

Asian Recorder. New Delhi: Asian Recorder, 1955—.

A weekly indexed digest of outstanding Asian events. It summarizes American, European, and Asian news dispatches. It is a ready source of information.

British Political Facts 1900-1979. 5th ed. David Butler and Anne Sloman. New York: St. Martin's Press, 1980.

Anglophiles, those who greatly admire British culture, will be delighted with this 500-page book of political facts on twentieth century British politics. It contains considerable biographical material conducive to studying the social backgrounds of British leaders. It also contains data on elections, civil service, royal commissions, administration of justice, social, labor, and economic conditions, royalty, the commonwealth, armed forces, the press, and a host of other topics.

China: A Handbook. Yuan-li Wu, ed. New York: Praeger, 1973.

With the renewal of Western contact with Mainland China, this volume of reference essays should be used by an increasing number of students. All the essays are by Western scholars, many of whom are of Chinese origin, however. They are detailed and scholarly, yet readable. Examples: "Sino-Soviet Relations," "Chinese Health and Medicine."

Canadian News Facts: The Indexed Digest of Canadian Current Events. Barrie Martland and Stephen D. Pepper, eds. Toronto, Ont.: Marpep, 1967—.

A twice-monthly publication that does in-depth wrapups on general news developments in the provincial capitals. It also covers foreign relations.

Commonwealth Political Facts. Chris Cook and John Paxton. London: Macmillan, 1979.

Commonwealth members include the United Kingdom, Canada, Australia, New Zealand, India, Sri Lanka, Ghana, Nigeria, Cyprus, Sierra Leone, Jamaica, Trinidad and Tobago, Uganda, Kenya, Malaysia, Tanzania, Malawi, Malta, Zambia, The Gambia, Singapore, Guyana, Botswana, Lesotho, Barbados, Mauritius, Swaziland, Tonga, Fiji, Western Somoa, Nauru, Bangladesh, Bahamas, Grenada, Papua, New Guinea, Seychelles, and their dependent territories. Former commonwealth member states are also listed. Factual data include: leaders of state over time, constitutions, ministers, elections, political parties, justice systems, defense and treaty obligations, populations and trade unions.

Countries of the World and Their Leaders Yearbook 1983. Detroit, Michigan: Gale Research Co., 1980—.

An annual compilation of U.S. Department of State, CIA, and other official reports on contemporary political and economic conditions of the countries of the world. It also contains the names of the chiefs of state and cabinet members of the governments of the world, list of nations, dependencies, and areas of special sovereignty, checklist of the newly independent nations, and other valuable data.

The East European and Soviet Data Handbook: Political, Social, and Developmental Indicators, 1945-1975. Paul S. Shoup. New York: Columbia University Press, 1981.

Covers the period 1945-1975, although it contains some information prior to World War II. It is designed to compare the communist countries of Eastern Europe and the Soviet Union on such levels as party membership, social classes, occupations, and educational levels. Also provides information on political leaders, but it does not contain economic statistics.

Electoral Behavior, A Comparative Handbook. Richard Rose. New York: The Free Press, 1974.

Today political behavior is no longer considered in isolation from socio-economic and cultural factors; this source summarizes such data from Western nations. Essays approach the frontier of the interdisciplinary study of political behavior. An article on Italy, for example, deals with social-psychological influences, contradictions in Italian political behavior, consumption patterns, and life-styles.

Encyclopedia of Latin Ameria. Helen Delpar. New York: McGraw-Hill, 1974.

A specialized source emphasizing the post-colonial or national period of Latin America. The topics themselves provide a good source of ideas for a paper, e.g., the history of women's political rights in Latin America.

Handbook of Latin American Studies. Dolores Mayano Martin, ed. Austin: University of Texas Press, 1936—.

Prepared by noted scholars for the Hispanic Division of the Library of Congress, this selective annotated guide to publications in the social sciences and humanities relating to Latin American affairs is currently in its 42nd volume. Volumes cover annual periods from 1935 to present and have been published by a number of university presses. A very fine guide for serious students of Latin America.

The International Relations of Eastern Europe: A Guide to Information Sources. Robin Alison Remington. Detroit, Mich.: Gale Research Company, 1978.

This well conceived bibliography is divided into two parts. Part 1 annotates books and articles on Eastern Europe as a region; part 2 is country specific. The countries are: Albania, Bulgaria, Czechoslovakia, East Germany, Hungary, Poland, Rumania, and Yugoslavia.

Keesing's Contemporary Archives: Weekly Indexed Diary of World Events. H. C. Tobin, and R. S. Fraser Keynsham, eds. Bristol, Eng.: Keesing's, 1931—.

These volumes are mainly a wrapup of news reports for each week, but they also include recent speeches and government documents, prominent obituaries, etc. This service covers world events but is strongest for the United Kingdom and Europe. It is indexed cumulatively into capsules of two weeks, three months, a year, and two years.

Marxist Governments: A World Survey. 3 vols. Bogdan Szajkowski, ed. London: Macmillan Press Ltd., 1981.

Twenty-five Marxist countries are surveyed by leading experts in the field. Each article is well-documented and each contains a fine bibliography which can be used in future research.

McGraw-Hill Encyclopedia of Russia and the Soviet Union. Michael T. Florinsky, ed. New York: McGraw-Hill, 1961.

Emphasizing events after 1918, this book contains detailed information on people and places, such as the Georgian Soviet Socialist Republic, not found elsewhere.

The Middle East. 5th ed. Washington, D.C.: Congressional Quarterly Inc., 1981.

One of Congressional Quarterly's public affairs books designed as a report on issues, events, and trends in this explosive region of the world. It examines U.S. involvement in the region, the arms races in the Middle East, and the potential for conflict between the superpowers. There is also a fine chapter on the history of Islam, and it contains biographies of key figures and profiles of countries in the region.

Middle East Record. The Reuven Shiloh Research Center of Tel Aviv University. Jerusalem, Israel: Israel Oriental Program for Scientific Translations, 1960—.

The Middle East continues to be an important area in world affairs, and often accounts of a particular event there differ. This source presents concise summaries of daily happenings from over 200 newspapers, periodicals, and official reports. When the Palestinian refugees exchange violence with the Israelis, one hears many versions of the incident. This source, with irregular publication, allows the researcher the single best opportunity to draw his own conclusion.

3f Political Events, Historic

These selected sources draw together key clusters of historical and political information. Most of the information is available elsewhere but these sources pull it all together in one convenient place along with helpful comments and analysis.

A Chronology and Fact Book of the United Nations, 1941–1964. Waldo Chamberlain and Thomas Hovet. Dobbs Ferry, N.Y.: Oceana, 1979.

A chronological listing of the important acts, events, meetings, membership, etc., of the UN, frequently with brief identifying statements.

Congressional Quarterly's Guide to U.S. Elections. Washington, D.C.: Congressional Quarterly Inc., 1975 (1977 paperback supplement).

This massive publication contains election data obtained from the Inter-University Consortium for Political Research (ICPR). It contains raw election return data and perceptive commentary for all major U.S. political offices from 1824 to 1975. A tremendous time-saver for student researchers interested in elections.

An Encyclopedia of World History: Ancient, Medieval, and Modern, Chronologically Arranged. rev. ed. William L. Langer, ed. Boston: Houghton Mifflin, 1972.

In no other volume can one locate the essential facts of world history so quickly. Using an expanded outline form with important names and dates in boldface type, this single volume covers the recorded history of the world. Extensively indexed, it allows one to expend a minimum of effort to find such data as the chronology of the short Soviet-Finnish war of 1939–1940 or the Moslem conquest of Spain in 711–1031.

European Political Facts 1789–1848. Chris Cook and John Paxton. New York: Facts on File, 1981.

European Political Facts 1848–1918. Chris Cook and John Paxton. London: Macmillan, 1978.

European Political Facts 1918–1973. Chris Cook and John Paxton. London: Macmillan, 1975.

These three volumes are similarly arranged books containing important political facts of all European countries from the Iberian west coast to the Tsarist and Ottoman empires of the East. Topics include areas such as the heads of state, election results, political parties, economic data, and much other information vital for serious students of European politics.

Foreign Relations of the United States: Diplomatic Papers. Washington, D.C.: Government Printing Office, 1861—.

A Department of State series that offers the most complete State Department records of the past. Published annually, these books contain a selection of public documents, diplomatic correspondence, messages between the United States and other governments, and departmental memoranda. The content is limited by omission for confidentiality and security as well as an approximately 25-year lag in publication.

Guide to American Foreign Relations Since 1700. Richard D. Burns, ed. Santa Barbara: ABC CLIO, 1983.

(Annotated in Chapter 4c.)

Historic Documents of 1981. Carolyn Goldinger, ed. Washington, D.C.: Congressional Quarterly, Inc., 1982.

Published each year since 1972, with future editions anticipated, these volumes contain documents of historical importance in chronological order.

For example, this volume contains President Carter's announcement of the release of the U.S. hostages in Iran and the texts of the Ottawa Economic Summit. Each entry is preceded by an introduction placing the document in perspective. The volumes are indexed for easy use.

Historical Atlas. 9th ed. Revised and updated. William Robert Shepherd, New York: Barnes & Noble, 1976.

A superb one-volume atlas covering the world from about 1945 B.C. to the near present. Each map is arranged chronologically (there is no accompanying text). It contains an exhaustive index of place names, including classical and medieval Latin place names, many of which do not appear on the maps. These are cross-referenced to the modern forms of the names.

History of U.S. Political Parties. Arthur M. Schlesinger, Jr., Gen. ed., 4 vols. New York: Chelsea House, 1973. Republished in paperback in 1980.

A massive one-stop source for a term paper on U.S. political parties, major and minor. After an introductory essay on each party, there are additional essays on the major sources in the field. For example, after an essay on the American Independent Party, this source reprints the party's 1968 platform, a press interview with George Wallace, and Governor Wallace's 1968 Madison Square Garden speech.

Issues Before the General Assemblies of the United Nations: 1946–1965. New York: Arno, 1970.

A specially compiled selection of excerpts from the major speeches and issues on the General Assembly agenda since its first session in 1946. Also compiled for this edition is a cumulative index that leads to one-source basic information concerning relevant problems facing the United Nations— a good first stop for a term paper.

National Party Platforms 1840–1976 (with 1980 supplement). Donald B. Johnson, comp. Urbana, Ill.: University of Illinois Press, 1982.

Even though a political party platform is not often adhered to once the elections are over, it must be considered an indicator of the goals and internal dissensions of the party. Included are the platforms of many minor parties, as well as those of the two major parties. For example, the 1960 platforms of the Democratic, Republican, Prohibition Socialist, Socialist, Labor, and Socialist Worker parties.

Nationalism and National Development: An Interdisciplinary Bibliography. Karl W. Deutsch and Richard L. Merritt. Cambridge, Mass.: MIT Press, 1970.

(Annotated in Chapter 2d.)

Summaries of Leading Cases on the Constitution. 11th ed. Paul C. Barthelomew, revised by Joseph F. Menez. Totowa, N.J.: Littlefield, Adams and Co., 1981.

Contains concise summaries of the most frequently cited and discussed cases since the establishment of the U.S. Supreme Court. Each case summary states the facts, legal issues, decisions, reasoning, and the division of the vote on the Supreme Court.

3g Political Events, Current

These sources summarize what is happening today. If one is totally lost as to where to start on a paper, these sources should be very helpful.

Congressional Quarterly Service

Although privately printed since 1945, the "CQ" series of publications has achieved the status of an official publication and is the most frequently cited source of governmental information. Its major attribute is its concise factual arrangement of material previously tucked away in bulky government documents.

The Congressional Quarterly publications present a careful review of each session of Congress in both legislative and political areas. Facts, figures, and unbiased commentary on all aspects of congressional activity are presented, including committee meetings and floor action. The President's position on all major legislation and roll-call votes in Congress are superimposed. Also included are the President's messages to Congress, his news conferences, his vetoes, and so on.

The basic publication is the *Congressional Quarterly Weekly Report.* From this report a yearly *Congressional Quarterly Almanac* is compiled.

Congressional Quarterly also publishes semi-annually a current handbook for the study of American government, the *Congressional Quarterly Guide to Current American Government,* which contains research material written and arranged for classroom and study use, as well as the *Editorial Research Reports,* a weekly publication that objectively assembles the facts involved in current controversial topics in well-researched and documented articles of about 6,000 words each. A library subscribing to the *Congressional Quarterly Weekly Report* probably receives the *Editorial Research Reports,* which also is annotated in this section.

The Basic Handbook Reference Series from Congressional Quarterly are: *America Votes: A Handbook of Contemporary American Election Statistics.* Richard M. Scammon, ed. Pittsburgh, Pa.: University of Pittsburgh Press, 1956–64. Washington, D.C.: Congressional Quarterly, 1966—.

(Annotated in Chapter 4a.)

Congress and the Nation, 1977–1980: A Review of Government and Politics.
Washington, D.C.: Congressional Quarterly Service, 1980.

These hardbound volumes document all major congressional and presidential actions and national political campaigns for the periods between 1945 and 1980. The first volume treats the years 1945–1964; the second, 1965–1968; the third, 1969–1972; the fourth, 1973–1976, and this, the latest, 1977–1980.

Congressional Quarterly's Guide to Congress. 3rd ed. Washington, D.C.: Congressional Quarterly, Inc., 1982.

A comprehensive reference guide on the history, procedures, politics, powers, and organization of the U.S. Congress. Packed with detailed information on all aspects of Congress and the political process.

Congressional Quarterly's Guide to U.S. Elections. Washington, D.C.: Congressional Quarterly Inc., 1975.

(Annotated in Chapter 3f.)

Congressional Quarterly's Guide to the U.S. Supreme Court. Washington, D.C.: Congressional Quarterly Inc., 1979.

Contains information on all aspects of the Supreme Court. Topics include the Court history; the Court and federalism; the Court and presidential power; the Court and judicial power; the Court and the states; the Court, civil liberties and rights; the political pressures on the Court; the internal operation of the Court; and major decisions of the Court.

Editorial Research Reports (Congressional Quarterly). Hoyt Gimlin, ed. Washington, D.C.: Congressional Quarterly, 1923—.

Issued weekly, this publication selects a major issue currently receiving public attention and assembles the facts. Each report starts with a recital of upcoming or recent developments. That is followed by an exposition of the main arguments on both sides and a list of the forces at work to change the situation. Also included are further background, historical development, and proposals for the future. Moreover, there are approximately 10 one-page summaries of other issues of the week. Although designed for newspaper editorial writers, *Editorial Research Reports* provides an excellent one-stop summary of current issues.

Federal Regulatory Directory. Washington, D.C.: Congressional Quarterly. 1979—.

This is a clear, concise, factual, easy-to-read, and useful guide to a major function of government. Includes an introductory chapter on regulation itself, then separate sections on both the independent regulatory agencies such as the Civil Aeronautics Board and the numerous regulatory units in major cabinet departments such as the Federal Railroad Administration in the Department

of Transportation. Entries bring together information on each agency's responsibilities, power and authority, organization, background information on
key members, legislation, important policies and issues.

Guide to the Congress of the United States: Origins, History, and Procedure.
2d ed. Washington, D.C.: Congressional Quarterly, 1976.
   An in-depth study of Congress, it is essentially factual and politically
oriented. It deals with both rules and procedures and how the various factions
have used them. It is the definitive factual source on Congress.

Washington Information Directory 1982-83. Washington, D.C.: Congressional Quarterly, Inc., 1982—.
   This annual publication is a comprehensive guide to U.S. government and
private information sources by subject. Contains detailed subject/agency and
organization index and provides the names, telephone numbers, addresses,
and responsibilities of information sources.

Paperback Series
   Congressional Quarterly also publishes a number of paperbacks which
focus on either a process such as *Mass Media and American Politics* or a policy
area such as *U.S. Defense Policy.* Each one of the following is likely the most
concise summary of the current issues to be found.
Candiates '84 (1984)
China: U.S. Policy Since 1945 (1980)
Congressional Ethics, 2nd ed. (1980)
Congressional Procedures and the Policy Process (1978)
Congressional Roll Call 1979—. Annual.
Elections 1982 (1982)
Energy Policy (1979)
Financing Politics, 2d ed. (1980)
Inside Congress, 2d ed. (1978)
Invitation to Struggle (1980)
Mass Media and American Politics (1980)
Members of Congress Since 1789 (1977)
Middle East, 4th ed. (1979)
National Party Conventions from 1831-1976 (1976)
Origins and Development of Congress (1975)
Politics in America (1979)
Politics of Drugs, 2d ed. (1980)
Powers of Congress (1976)
President Carter 1979 (1979)
President Reagan 1981 (1981)
Presidential Elections Since 1789, 2nd ed. (1979)
Supreme Court and Individual Rights (1980)

Taxes, Jobs, and Inflation (1979)
U. S. Defense Policy, 3d ed. (1983)
Urban America (1979)
Washington Lobby, 3rd ed. (1979)

Facts on File: Weekly World News Digest with Cumulative Index. New York:
Facts on File, Inc., 1940—.
This publication records the events of each week of a given year in an
unbiased and concise style. Each news item is filed and reported under a
specific heading such as world affairs, national affairs, sports, and the like.
Each also includes a reference to any previous article on the same topic.
However, sources are not listed. There are cumulative monthly, semi-annual,
and yearly indexes.

Keesing's Contemporary Archives: Weekly Indexed Diary of World Events.
H. C. Tobin and R. S. Fraser Keynsham, eds. Bristol, Eng.: Keesing's, 1931—.
Mainly a wrapup of news reports for each week, but the volumes also
include recent speeches and government documents, prominent obituaries,
etc. The service covers world events but is strongest for the United Kingdom
and Europe. It is indexed cumulatively into capsules of two weeks, three
months, a year, and two years.

National Journal. Burt Hoffman, ed. Washington, D.C.: Center for Political
Research, 1970—.
Titled *National Journal Reports* from July 28, 1973 to Aug. 16, 1975. It
was founded by a group of editors and reporters who left Congressional
Quarterly because they felt it did not pay enough attention to bureaucratic
decision making. The *Journal* is published weekly and designed as a monitor
of all government actions. It does more than record government actions; it
analyzes all the details surrounding such actions, focusing mainly on the
relationships between the various power-wielding agencies that cram the
nation's capital. The interests involved in any issue are plainly identified—
this, in itself, cuts away much of the mystery for the student. It also contains
in-depth reports on federal programs, biographical information on government
officials, and analyses of congressional districts.

3h BIOGRAPHIC MATERIAL

Biographic accounts of individual lives vary considerably in depth and
focus. The following sources include:
1. In-depth studies, usually written after the subject has died, ex. *Dictionary of American Biography.*
2. Brief factual sketches, *International Yearbook and Statesman's Who's Who.*

3. Journalistic summaries, brief sketches combining basic facts with some interpretation, ex. *Current Biography*.
4. Monographs.
5. Special topical focuses which emphasize either a particular aspect of the subjects' lives, ex. *American Assassins*, or a special type of material, ex. *Treasury of Presidential Quotations*.

It is possible to use biographical material as a prime source for a paper, *e.g.*, comparing the twentieth century senators from a given state. It is also possible to use it as a check against other sources.

American Assassins. Jo Anne Ray. Minneapolis, Minn.: Lerner, 1974.

Unfortunately, assassins are significant political actors on the American scene. This work contains biographies of significant assassins and would-be assassins from John Wilkes Booth to Sirhan Sirhan.

American State Governors 1776–1976. 2 volumes. Joseph E. Kallenbach and Jessamine S. Kallenbach. Dobbs Ferry, N.Y.: Oceana Publications, 1981.

Currently available in two of three planned volumes, the authors present in narrative form biographical information of the nearly 1,100 individuals who held gubernatorial office from Alabama to Montana. Employed together with Roy R. Glashan's *American Governors and Gubernatorial Elections, 1775–1978*, students have available a wealth of information which previously had not been readily accessible.

American Governors and Gubernatorial Elections, 1775–1978. Roy R. Glashan. Westport, Conn.: Meckler Books, 1979.

This excellent source book for studying state chief executives is arranged alphabetically by name of state. It contains short biographies of each governor for each state and territory dating from 1775 to 1978. Biographical data include: birthdate, birthplace, residence, occupation, party affiliation, date of death, and date and age on assuming office. Also included are statistics for all gubernatorial elections. This one volume can be used in conjunction with the two-volume set covering the same topic, *American Governors 1776–1976* by Kallenbach and Kallenbach.

Biographical Directory of United States Executive Branch 1774–1977. Robert Sobel, ed. Westport, Conn.: Greenwood Publications, 1977.

In addition to biographies of over 500 cabinet-level officials from colonial days to the recent past, this book includes useful comparative tables indicating level of education and college attended, birthplace, and so forth. One could thus easily find all federal officials who had attended a particular college or had been born in a specific city or town.

Biography Index. New York: H. W. Wilson, 1947—.
(Annotated in Chapter 2f.)

Congress Biographical Directory, 1774-1971. Washington, D.C.: Government Printing Office, 1972.
(Annotated in Chapter 4d.)

Congressional Directory. Washington, D.C.: Government Printing Office, 1809—.
(Annotated in Chapter 4d.)

Congressional Staff Directory. Charles B. Brownson, ed. Mount Vernon, Va.: Congressional Staff Director, 1959—.
(Annotated in Chapter 4d.)

Current Biography. New York: H. W. Wilson, 1940—.
Current Biography supplies unbiased, well written sketches of contemporary personalities in about 40 different professional fields. The emphasis is upon figures in the news. The biographies are based mostly upon current news articles that H. W. Wilson indexes. The book contains photographs of each subject, gives the proper pronunciation of the more difficult names, and lists references to additional material. Each issue contains an accrued-list index of the previous issues. Besides the annual compilation, there are 10-year indexes.

Current World Leaders. International Academy at Santa Barbara, Santa Barbara, California.
The "Almanac Issue" is published three times a year and lists key officials of all independent states, international organizations and alliances. The "Biograph and News Speeches and Reports Issue" is published five times a year and brings together general background information, biographies, speeches from several viewpoints and official reports from each country.

Dictionary of American Biography. New York: Charles Scribner, 1928–1977, with supplements.
A product of the American Council of Learned Societies, this multivolume work differs from most biographical entities in that its entries are balanced essays written after the death of the subjects—not just a collection of facts. The emphasis in the main volumes is naturally upon nineteenth-century figures. More recent supplements concentrate on figures from the 1930s and 1940s. The essay on Harry Hopkins, for example, explains Hopkins' profound impact on the development of American social welfare and World War II diplomacy and tells how his early experience shaped his ideas.

Encyclopedia of American Biography. John A. Garraty, ed. New York: Harper & Row, 1974.
The first half of each 500-word entry in this book is a factual biographical sketch. The second half is an assessment of the individual's whole career

(although many of the subjects are still living) by someone with specialized knowledge on the subject. This is followed by a biographical reference. Interpretations are bound to be controversial, but one may find the volume useful for just that reason. The two-paragraph assessments may provide a good jumping off point for defining a proposition about the subject.

The Enigma of Felix Frankfurter. H. N. Hirsch. New York: Basic Books, 1981.

An example of psychobiography. Focuses upon the personality of this controversial Associate Justice of the U.S. Supreme Court. The author analyzes Frankfurter as a liberal New Dealer and how he became an isolated figure on the Supreme Court.

Facts About the Presidents. Joseph Nathan Kane. New York: H. W. Wilson, 1976—.

This is a thorough compilation of biographical and historical data including much information not usually assembled, such as number of brothers and sisters, key appointments, and important firsts.

International Encyclopedia of the Social Sciences: Biographical Supplement. David L. Sills, ed. New York: The Free Press, 1979.

This source takes its place as volume 18 in the set titled *International Encyclopedia of the Social Sciences* (annotation in Chapter 3k.) It tells the life stories and describes the academic contributions of some noted social scientists. As the editor David Sills points out, the more we know about the life and times of a scholar the better able we may be to understand his contributions. The disciplines covered are broadly defined to include history, human biology, religion and statistics as well as the more commonly understood social science disciplines. Biographies of notables in political science and legal theory include: Hannah Arendt, Alexander Bickel, Edward S. Corwin, David Fellman, Paul A. Freund, Carl J. Friedrich, John S. Furnivall, Pendleton Herring, Philip C. Jessup, Bertrand De Jovenel, George F. Kennan, Hans Kohn, Harold D. Lasswell, Gerhard Leibholz, Myers S. McDougal, Hans J. Morgenthau, E. E. Schattschneider, Harold and Margaret Spout, Leo Strauss, Carl B. Swisher, Eric Voegelin, Karl A. Wittfogel, and Quincy Wright.

International Who's Who. London: Europa Publications, 1935—.

Published annually since 1935, this reference contains from 8,000 to 13,000 biographical sketches on prominent figures of the world. The *International Who's Who* provides brief but reliable information on the subjects, giving name, title, dates, nationality, education, profession, career, works, and addresses.

International Yearbook and Statesmen's Who's Who. East Grinstead, West Sussex, England: Kelly's Directories, 1953—.

Until 1973 this yearbook was published by Burke's Peerage in London. It combines data on political and economic conditions of the world with an international biographical directory of about 10,000 individuals of world renown: statesmen, diplomats, military leaders, clergy, industrialists, and so forth. The information on various nations, arranged alphabetically, is similar to that in the *Statesman's Yearbook* but with more statistical details.

The Justices of the United States Supreme Court 1789-1969: Their Lives and Major Opinions, 5 vols. Leon Friedman and Fred L. Israel, eds. New York and London: Chelsea House Publishers, 1969, 1978.

A massive effort to record the lives and important opinions of every member of the Supreme Court from 1789 to 1978. It is the most complete work of its kind and provides a valuable bibliography of available articles and books on each Supreme Court justice.

Lyndon Johnson and the American Dream. Doris Kearns. New York: Harper and Row, 1976.

A penetrating account of the personality and behavior of the complex person who gave his countrymen the Great Society and the War in Vietnam. It examines his private and public life from his early years through his years in the U.S. Senate and his Presidency.

Madmen and Geniuses: The Vice-Presidents of the United States. Sol Barzman. Chicago: Follett, 1974.

One-third of our presidents have been vice-presidents. Each of them is described in terms of his background and later career in office.

The McGraw-Hill Encyclopedia of World Biography, 12 vols. New York: McGraw-Hill, 1973.

Contains well written articles about 5,000 significant individuals. The emphasis is upon less known Third World figures and leaders. The book is useful because the articles explain *why* particular figures were chosen for discussion. The articles are in narrative form, go beyond a recitation of facts, and include many illustrations.

Modern World Rulers: A Chronology. Alan R. Langville, compiler. Metuchen, N.J.: Scarecrow Press, Inc., 1979.

A listing of the heads of state and government for all independent nation-states since 1800. Also lists state and provincial leaders for the U.S. and Canada.

New York Times Biographical Service. vol. 8. New York: Arno Press, 1977—.

Until this edition, the title was *New York Times Biographical Editions, Reprints on Biographical Material* (1969—). A weekly collection of all the biographical material in the *New York Times.* This includes obituaries as well as full-length personality sketches.

Notable American Women 1607-1950. A Biographical Dictionary. Edward T. James, Janet Wilson James, and Paul S. Boyer, eds. Cambridge, Mass.: Belknap Press of Harvard University Press, 1971; *Notable American Women: The Modern Period: A Biographical Dictionary.* Barbara Sicherman, Carol Hurd Green, Ilene Kantrov, Harnette Walker, eds. Cambridge, Mass.: Belknap Press of Harvard University Press, 1980. Important because these works identify many women who have made significant contributions in many fields but have not gained historical recognition.

Politics in America: Members of Congress in Washington and at Home, 1982. Alan Ehrenhalt, ed. Washington, D.C.: Congressional Quarterly, Inc., 1981.

Excellent profiles of the 535 members of the U.S. House of Representatives and Senate. Contains analyses of each congressional district and elections, voting studies, key votes, interest group ratings and other relevant information on the Congress and its members. Future editions are expected.

Who's Who in America: A Biographical Dictionary of Notable Living Men and Women. Chicago: A. N. Marquis, 1899—.

Subjects of these biographies fall into two groups: those selected because of their special prominence or distinction in certain fields, and those included arbitrarily because of their official position or public standing. Included are persons of all nationalities who are likely to be of interest to Americans. It is supplemented by *Who Was Who in America*, for all persons deleted because of death; *The Monthly Supplement*, December 1939 to 1956; the *Supplement to Who's Who*, issued quarterly since 1957; the *Ten-Year Cumulative Index, 1939-1949;* and the *Cumulative Index for 1951-1955*. The major publication is revised and reissued biennially.

Who's Who in American Politics. 8th ed. Jaques Cattel Press, ed., 1981. New York: R. R. Bowker.

First published to cover the 1973-74 period, this work is a biographical directory of thousands of political leaders in the United States. It is a thorough and authoritative publication that is edited jointly by officials of both major parties. The biographical material was gathered mostly by questionnaires, but the editors note in the introduction that in some cases, when they felt the prominence of the biographee warranted inclusion even though his or her questionnaire was not returned, they gathered the necessary data themselves. Biographical data were culled from various sources, and the biographee was asked to verify a proof copy before the information was included in the directory.

3i Quotations & Speeches

The Chief Executive-Inaugural Addresses of the President of the United States, from George Washington to Lyndon B. Johnson. Introduction by Arthur Schlesinger, Commentary by Fred L. Israel, conceived and ed. by Chelsea House Publishers, New York: Crown, 1965.

The commentaries are especially helpful because they present the historical context of and major issues behind each speech.

Familiar Quotations: A Collection of Passages, Phrases, and Proverbs Traced to Their Sources in Ancient and Modern Literature. John Bartlett, ed. Boston: Little, Brown, 1980—.

A useful collection of thousands of quotations that have become part of the English language. Bartlett lists each quotation under its author and reprints it within the context of the poem, passage, or article as it originally appeared. The authors are listed chronologically, and there is a topical index referring to page and author. For instance, the source of the line, "What this country needs is a good five-cent cigar," can be found under *cigar* in the line index. (The source of this quotation, incidentally, is Thomas R. Marshall, vice-president under Woodrow Wilson.)

The Presidents Speak: The Inaugural Addresses of the American Presidents, from Washington to Nixon. 3rd ed. Annotated by Davis Newton Lott. New York: Holt, Rinehart & Winston, 1969.

The annotations are especially helpful because they highlight key ideas and comparisons to other presidents.

Treasury of Presidential Quotations. Caroline Harnsberger. Chicago: Follett, 1964.

Thomas Jefferson said, "Indeed I tremble for my country when I reflect that God is just." This and other presidential quotations are organized under specialized subject headings in this source.

Vital Speeches of the Day. New York: City News, 1934—.

This monthly journal prints the verbatim text of important speeches by recognized leaders of public opinion in America. Generally, it covers both sides of public questions, thereby offering the significant thought of leading minds on current national problems. The journal explains that its purpose is to offer students "the finest textbook material . . . from those who have attained leadership in the fields of politics, economics, education, sociology, government, criminology, finance, business, taxation, health, law, labor. . . ."

What They Said in ——. Beverly Hills, Calif.: Monitor, 1969—.

The most recent publication of this work was in 1979, covering the previous year. In this work, current lively and interesting quotes by public figures are arranged according to topics. Thus, one can look up what others have said about "Asia and the Pacific" or look up individual figures such as Jimmy Carter to see what he said on a particular topic in recent years.

Who Said What (and When and Where and How) in 1971, Vol. 1 Jan.-June. Barbara Bennett and Linda Amster. New York: Quadrangle, 1972—.

This source is really based on who said what in the *New York Times*. Quotations are arranged by subject with reference to the *Times* edition in which it appeared. There is an extensive index. It is useful for tracking down fugitive quotations.

U.S. Presidents, The State of the Union Messages of the Presidents, 1790–1966. Fred L. Israel, ed. 3 vols. New York: Chelsea House, 1966.

An introductory essay by Arthur Schlesinger, Jr., suggests themes and points upon which to compare various presidents. The subject index can be very useful.

3j DICTIONARIES AND GLOSSARIES

A dictionary is a book that explains the agreed-upon meanings of words. The word glossary usually applies to a list of such words, terms, or phrases in a particular subject area. The following dictionaries and glossaries vary in several important ways:

1. Some focus on straightforward definitions of political terms and their contemporary significance, *e.g.*, the *American Political Dictionary*.
2. Some offer longer philosophic and analytic discussions of words and terms. These dictionaries are a source in themselves and some, such as *Safire's Political Dictionary*, are very enjoyable to read.
3. Some are specialized in a particular area of political science, *e.g.*, *A Dictionary of Modern Revolutions*.

Dictionaries are unlikely to be a prime source for a term paper but they may provide background and context to your basic material. They are also useful if one finds the instructor seems to be making frequent references to unfamiliar people, places, events, concepts, and ideas. In such cases a special political dictionary can teach the terms quickly.

The following Clio dictionaries in political science are published by ABC-Clio, Santa Barbara, Calif.: 1980–83:

> *The African Political Dictionary*
>   Claude S. Phillips
> *The International Relations Dictionary. 3rd ed.*
>   Jack C. Plano and Roy Olton
> *The Latin American Political Dictionary*
>   Ernest E. Rossi and Jack C. Plano
> *The Middle East Political Dictionary*
>   Lawrence Ziring
> *The Soviet and East European Political Dictionary*
>   George Klein, Barbara P. McCrea, and Jack C. Plano

Acronyms, Initialisms, & Abbreviations Dictionary. 7th ed. Ellen Crowley, ed. Detroit: Gale Research Co., 1980. Formerly titled *Acronyms and Initialisms Dictionary* (4th ed., 1973).

During approximately the last 20 years rapid changes in technology and world events have given us new ways of identifying already familiar persons (JFK, LBJ, etc.) as well as many new political organizations and slogans that have never been known by anything but their acronyms: COMSAT (Communications Satellite Corporation); GOO (Get Oil Out of Santa Barbara): NOW (The National Organization for Women); OWL (Older Women's Liberation). The nationally prominent and the obscure, the profound and the humorous—this reference contains them all.

The American Political Dictionary. 6th ed. Jack C. Plano and Milton Greenberg. New York: Holt, Rinehart and Winston, 1982.

This paperback book contains more than 1,200 key terms, agencies, court cases, and statutes particularly relevant to the study of American government and politics. Each one-paragraph definition is followed by a paragraph outlining its contemporary significance.

American Political Terms: An Historical Dictionary. Hans Sperber and Travis Trittschuh. Detroit: Wayne State University Press, 1962.

Differs from the above dictionaries in that it emphasizes the historical derivation of terms. For example, this dictionary shows how the term *silk stocking* as it refers to the wealthy elite, was used by Thomas Jefferson in 1812 and has been used since by numerous others. When using this dictionary, one would probably not be looking up "long hair" because one did not know what the term meant but rather because one would like to know the origin of the term in American politics. In this instance, the authors note references to long-haired radicals at the time of the Civil War, and then they trace the use of the phrase to the near present.

Black's Law Dictionary: Definition of Terms and Phrases of American and English Jurisprudence, Ancient and Modern. 5th ed. St. Paul, Minn.: West, 1979.

The definitive law dictionary. Since legal terms are often part of political controversy, it is helpful to have access to precise definitions of such terms as "indeterminate sentence," "covenant," and "beyond a reasonable doubt."

Dictionary of American Biography. New York: Charles Scribner, 1928–1958, with supplements.

(Annotated in Chapter 3h.)

Dictionary of American Diplomatic History. John E. Findling. Westport, Conn.: Greenwood Press, 1980.

Contains over 1,000 entries on U.S. diplomatic history from the Revolution to the contemporary period. Each entry is accompanied by references for additional study.

A Dictionary of Concepts on American Politics. James B. Whisker. New York: John Wiley and Sons, 1980.

A good dictionary of concepts, it is most likely to be encountered by undergraduates in American government courses. Concepts are arranged by subject matter, such as the court system, the presidency, and Congress.

Dictionary of the History of Ideas: Studies of Selected Pivotal Ideas. Philip P. Wiener, ed. New York: Charles Scribner, 1973.

Although many of the entries fall outside the realm of politics, there are many that deal in a multidisciplinary fashion with a number of key political concepts. "Authority," for example, is traced from ancient times to the present, and the many issues raised by the concept are thoroughly examined.

A Dictionary of Modern Revolutions. Edward S. Hyams. New York: Taplinger, 1973.

The authors quote Baudelaire, who said, "Life being what it is, one dreams of revenge." This is a guide to how these dreams have become a reality. The entries tend to be long and philosophical, ranging from Marx to the Soledad Brothers.

A Dictionary of Modern War. Edward Luttwak, New York: Harper & Row, 1971.

This work includes both technical terms such as "bloodhound" (a British missile) and conceptual terms with a precise military meaning such as "threshold" (a demarcation line between particular levels of violence between states).

A Dictionary of Political Analysis. Geoffrey Roberts. New York: St. Martin's Press, 1971.

Emphasizes methodological terms, concepts such as "black box technique," forms of organization, categories, and political ideologies; it mostly excludes concrete references such as court cases, names, places, and events.

A Dictionary of Politics. rev. ed. Walter Laqueur, ed. New York: The Free Press, 1974.

This dictionary emphasizes factual events from recent history rather than philosophical meanings. For example, in this book one can find the political meaning of "Little Rock, Arkansas," the "Subversive Activities Control Board," the "Kennedy Round," or "Maxim Litinov."

Dictionary of Politics: Selected American and Foreign Political and Legal Terms. 6th ed. Lawrenceville, Va.: Brunswick Publishing Co., 1978.

With over 4,600 entries this volume defines political and legal concepts, terms, and references; also contains appendixes on subjects such as the distribution of electoral votes by states and the Laffer curve (the backbone of Reaganomics).

A Glossary of Political Ideas. Maurice Cranston and Sanford A. Lakoff. New York: Basic Books, 1969.

An unusually useful source for starting a term paper. Over 50 key ideas are explained and analyzed. Liberalism, for example, has meant different things at different times from the era of John Stuart Mill to recent times.

This volume traces these meanings and then presents a short bibliography for further reference.

A Guide to Communist Jargon. Robert N. C. Hunt. New York: Macmillan, 1957.

Consists of in-depth essays that thoroughly explore the meanings of terms as used by communist (mostly Soviet) writers. "Cosmopolitanism," for instance, is considered a reactionary force of international feeling because it urges people to renounce their struggle for national independence. This guide may also be used as a primer on communist ideology.

The Language of Cities: A Glossary of Terms. Charles Abrams. New York: Viking, 1971.

Emphasizes terms in the areas of urban renewal, land use, planning, and community politics. It shows how the forces of history, economics, and government programs have all combined to develop a new "language." For example, the entry on urban personality will help explain why urbanites behave as they do.

News Dictionary. New York: Facts on File, 1964—.

An unusual source. One simply looks up the topic to find out what happened in that area over the past year. For example, "Hijackings" provides a concise summary of all hijackings by country for the year.

Notable American Women 1607-1950. A Biographical Dictionary. Edward T. James, Janet Wilson James, and Paul S. Boyer, eds. Cambridge, Mass.: Belknap Press of Harvard University Press, 1971.

(Annotated in Chapter 3h.)

Political Science Thesaurus II. rev. 2d ed. Carl Beck, Thomas McKechnie, and Paul Evan Peters. Pittsburgh: University Center for International Studies, University of Pittsburgh in conjunction with the American Political Science Association, 1979.

When writing a paper, students often want to find a different word for one that has already been used or used too often. This thesaurus contains thousands of such words. For example, if you are writing about "power politics" you may find the following useful substitutions: "Realpolitik," "realist foreign policy," "conflict theory," and others.

Primer on Constitutional Law. Albert P. Melone and Carl Kalvelage. Pacific Palisades, Calif.: Palisades Publishers, 1982.

Chapter 5 contains a glossary of terms and phrases employed in the constitutional law field of study.

Safire's Political Dictionary. William Safire. New York: Random House, 1978.
   This is an enlarged, up-dated edition of *The New Language of Politics: An Anecdotal Dictionary of Catchwords, Slogans and Political Usage.* William Safire. New York: Collier, 1972. It provides the origin of such phrases as "dirty tricks department." The author is a newspaper columnist, practicing politician, and former Nixon staffer. A fascinating essay on the origins of political terms precedes the body of the work. Especially interesting in this essay are all the new terms that have emerged since the first printing of the work in 1968. For example, if a paper is dealing with changing political ideas, campaigns, or programs, a reading of the 12 pages from "new political use of" through "new politics" will enable one to write with much more perception and clarity about political change.

3k ENCYCLOPEDIAS

An encyclopedia is a scholarly work which contains objective articles on subjects in every field of knowledge within its scope. Most people instinctively turn to a general reference encyclopedia as their first source of reference, as this is the most convenient source of quick information in the library. A good encyclopedia contains not only a great deal of important substantive information but also useful bibliographies, cross references, and other guides to help in conducting further research.

Although the term *encyclopedia* denotes an all-inclusive approach, even encyclopedias specialize. We have annotated a number of specialized encyclopedias which political science students will find particularly applicable.

African Encyclopedia. London: Oxford University Press, 1974.
   (Annotated in Chapter 3e.)

American Jurisprudence, 2d. Rochester, N.Y.: The Lawyers Co-Operative Publishing Company and Bancroft-Whitney Company, 1962—(updated continually).
   A discussion of both substantive and procedural aspects of American law arranged in more than 400 title headings. This particular legal encyclopedia places great emphasis upon federal statutory law and federal procedural rules. Special procedures are required to use this and other legal encyclopedias. For a full discussion of these procedures, see Albert P. Melone and Carl Kalvelage, *Primer on Constitutional Law* (Pacific Palisades, Calif.: Palisades Publishers, 1982), pp. 8–17.

Collier's Encyclopedia. New York: Macmillan Educational Corp., 1981.
   Formerly published under the same title by Crowell-Collier and Macmillan, 1949, this is a strong, clearly written, well indexed, yearly-revised, general encyclopedia. It is reliable and often has sufficient depth for freshmen and sophomore assignments, although it is not exhaustive. It is a good first source with excellent bibliographies and indexes.

Compton's Pictured Encyclopedia and Fact-Index. Chicago: Encyclopedia Britannica, 1922—.

Compton's with yearly revisions is a good all-around reference source. Although it does not attempt to provide the depth of the *Britannica* or the *Americana,* it is especially helpful as a first reference source, and the articles are well written and fully keyed to school curricula. There are extensive bibliographies grouped for different educational levels. Each volume has a fact index leading the reader to a large selection of short factual and biographical entries.

The Encyclopedia Americana. Danbury, Conn.: Grolier, 1982—.

Formerly published (under the same title) by Americana Corp, 1829—, this is the strongest source for all aspects of American life and culture including, of course, American politics. Articles are written by leading scholars, with especially strong coverage of recent American history. The bibliography is extensive and so authoritative that it is frequently consulted by librarians. Revised yearly.

Encyclopedia of American Foreign Policy. 3 volumes. Charles Scribners, New York: 1978.

The focus of this work is ideas rather than facts and data. Composed of 4-to-10 page analytical essays on such topics as the military industrial complex, the behavioral approach to diplomatic history, and dissent in wars.

Encyclopedia of Associations. 18th ed. Denise S. Akey, ed. Detroit: Gale Research, 1983.

Alex de Tocqueville gave Americans an early clue about our tendency to form associations of all kinds, "religious, moral, serious, futile, restricted, enormous or diminutive." This three-volume work is evidence that the tendency is still there. Associations are broken down by type, with a geographic and executive index. Each entry includes purpose, activities, and publications. A section on public affairs organizations is of particular interest.

Encyclopedia of Government Advisory Organizations. Linda E. Sullivan, 3rd ed. Detroit: Gale Research, 1980.

Formerly titled, *Encyclopedia of Government Advisory Agencies.* Linda E. Sullivan and Anthony T. Kruzas, eds. Detroit: Gale, 1973. Political scientists have long been interested in the unique role of advisory agencies. Do they control the organizations they advise? Are they a vehicle for special interests? This work lists numerous interagency and related boards, committees, etc., their members, origins, and affiliations.

Encyclopedia International. New York: Grolier, 1981.

It is difficult to publish a new encyclopedia that can compete in scope and quality with the established sets, but with yearly revisions the *Encyclopedia International* is doing just that. It is a general encyclopedia similar to *Compton's* and *Collier's.* It is especially readable, with unusual headings and subheadings that heighten reader interest; it also includes such helpful and practical information as lists of colleges, study aids, and career guides.

Encyclopedia of Latin America. Helen Delpar. New York: McGraw-Hill, 1974.
   (Annotated in Chapter 3e.)

Encyclopedia of the Third World. 2 volumes. George Thomas Kurian. New York: Facts on File, 1979.
   Most scholars would agree with the author that the "Third World" may be "defined as the politically nonaligned and economically developing and less industrialized nations of the world." Given this definition, the author provides valuable information on 114 countries, including location, weather, population, ethnic composition, languages, religions, colonial experience, constitution and government, civil service, foreign policy, political parties, economy, and a variety of other information difficult to obtain in one source. This set also contains valuable comparative statistical tables of a political nature and a selective bibliography. Students conducting research on the Third World will find much data and bibliographic information conducive to writing a good paper.

Encyclopedia of Philosophy. Paul Edwards, ed. New York: Macmillan, 1967.
   Many political philosophers concern themselves with questions in such areas as ethics, scientific method, and the nature of reality. To understand their political ideas, it is often helpful to view other areas of their thought. This in-depth source helps with lengthy and scholarly articles. Might be difficult for the beginner.

Encyclopedia of the Social Sciences. E.R.A. Seligman and Alvin Johnson, eds. 15 vols. New York: Macmillan, 1930–35. Reprinted, 1962.
   Hundreds of international scholars prepared this comprehensive survey of the fields of social science in the early 1930s. They produced a work that was considered the most important in the field. It is no longer in print, having been superseded by the *International Encyclopedia of the Social Sciences.* However, many of the articles are classics in their field and can still fill a need in a paper stressing the development of ideas.

An Encyclopedia of World History: Ancient, Medieval, and Modern, Chronologically Arranged. rev. ed. William L. Langer, ed. Boston: Houghton Mifflin, 1972.
   (Annotated in Chapter 3f.)

The Great Ideas: A Syntopicon of Great Books of the Western World. Mortimer J. Adler, ed. Chicago: Encyclopedia Britannica, 1955.
   The two-volume *Syntopicon* contains an analytic essay for each of the 102 "great ideas." These essays break down and analyze each idea, illustrating in the process the intellectual elements of each. Under "law," for instance,

is a clear and succinct approach to the idea of law-divine and natural law, and the relationship of law and the individual. The remaining 54 volumes contain the works of the great thinkers and writers of Western civilization. To these 54 volumes the essays of the *Syntopicon* are keyed, permitting one to trace the development of an idea through history or to compare the views of two or more giants of history. Each of the 102 essays is cross-indexed, providing innumerable approaches to a single subject.

International Encyclopedia of the Social Sciences. David L. Sills, ed. 18 vols. New York: Macmillan and the Free Press, 1979.

These volumes constitute an exhaustive updating of the *Encyclopedia of the Social Sciences.* The set contains hundreds of articles by the world's leading social scientists, each article defining an entire field of study. The 18 volumes include a 349-page introduction in two parts: (1) A discussion of the meaning of the social sciences and an outline of their chronological development; and (2) a nation-by-nation survey of the disciplines involved in the social sciences. The main portion of the work deals with important concepts in political science, economics, law, anthropology, sociology, penology, and social work. About a quarter of the work is composed of biographical sketches. All entries are alphabetically listed with cross references and a subject index.

The McGraw-Hill Encyclopedia of World Biography. 12 vols. New York: McGraw-Hill, 1973.

(Annotated in Chapter 3h.)

Mraxism, Communism, and Western Society: A Comparative Encyclopedia. C. D. Kernig, ed. New York: Herder and Herder, 1972.

Emphasizes individual articles showing that differences exist between East and West. One can see the political meaning of topics usually considered nonpolitical—for example, the Soviet view toward art or the Soviet view of the Western policy of anticommunism.

The New Encyclopedia Britannica. 15th ed. Chicago: Encyclopedia Britannica, 1980.

The word *new* is certainly appropriate for this encyclopedia. The entire work has been massively reorganized and is actually two encyclopedias plus a one-volume outline of knowledge.

1. The Propedia is a one-volume outline of knowledge and a guide to the encyclopedia. It is, in effect, a table of contents for the rest of the work with introductory essays on the main areas of knowledge.
2. The Micropedia is a 10-volume ready reference encyclopedia. No article in it is longer than 750 words. It is useful for facts, names, dates, and quick explanations.
3. The Macropedia is intended to contain knowledge in depth. It consists of extensive essays, which one reads for education as well as for information. Some of the essays are excellent, and this source is especially worth investigating if the longer articles are relevant to a topic. For

example, the five-page essay on "Political Power" delineates the various applications of the term, the context of power, leadership, power in groups, and community power structures. There is also a good working bibliography that could be developed into many topics for a paper.

Worldmark Encyclopedia of Nations. 5th ed. New York: Worldmark Press, distributed by John Wiley and Sons, 1976.

This five-volume work presents geographic, social, historical, and political facts concerning the various nations of the world in an easy-to-use form. There are large standard subheadings, so one, for instance, may compare the transportation systems in Nigeria and Morocco quickly and easily.

4

Original Sources

As discussed in Chapter One, depending on the focus of the paper virtually any source can be utilized as originals. This chapter outlines three particular kinds of sources which are often overlooked or underutilized by political science students, government documents, data bases, and academic journals.

DATA SOURCES, POLLS, AND QUANTITATIVE APPLICATIONS

The political science profession has become increasingly competent and comfortable with the use of quantitative data and techniques in research. Today, students are often asked to collect their own information which can be translated into numbers and then analyzed with statistical tools. Statistical packages, which simplify the counting procedures, are now widely available; these "canned" computer packages may be used to perform statistical manipulations on either student generated data or data obtained through data archive centers.

There is a certain excitement in generating a data base from the planning stage to the collection of the raw information and then to proceed to statistical manipulation and finally to data interpretation. But it is not always necessary to generate one's own data. A number of data bases or sources are readily available to students. This section is intended to expose students to available data sources and to direct them to additional related materials. It includes data and statistics in traditional book form, and special sections on opinion polls and quantitative applications.

4a Data Sources

American Governors and Gubernatorial Elections 1775-1978. Roy R. Glashan. Westport, Conn.: Meckler Books, 1979.
(Annotated in Chapter 3h.)

American Social Attitudes Data Sourcebook: 1947-1978. Philip E. Converse, Jean E. Dotson, Wendy J. Hoag, and William H. McGee III. Cambridge, Mass.: Harvard University Press, 1980.

A very interesting compilation of poll results taken from the archives of the Survey Research Center at the University of Michigan. The authors have culled sample survey items that have been repeated a number of times since World War II. Thus, students can analyze the extent to which public opinion has changed over time concerning such topics as how much the government should spend on defense, education, and welfare. A large list of other social issues is available for time series analysis.

American National Election Studies Data Sourcebook, 1952-1978. Warren E. Miller, Arthur H. Miller, and Edward J. Schneider. Cambridge, Mass.: Harvard University Press, 1980.

Students of American voting behavior will treasure this sourcebook. It contains the results of the same or similar survey questions asked Americans from 1952 to 1972 by scholars located at the Center for Political Studies of the University of Michigan. It is now easily possible to ascertain changes over time for such factors as division of party loyalties within the electorate, political involvement and voter turnout, support measures, and a host of often discussed variables employed when explaining voting behavior.

American Statistics Index. Washington, D.C.: Congressional Information Service, 1972—.

(Annotated in Chapter 2f.)

America Votes: A Handbook of Contemporary American Election Statistics. Richard M. Scammon, ed. Pittsburgh, Pa.: University of Pittsburgh Press, 1956-64. Washington, D.C.: Congressional Quarterly, 1966—.

This is a prodigious biennial collection of voting statistics; it covers all the national elections from 1954 to the present, state by state. The detailed vote breakdown includes national, state, and county election statistics. State and county figures include total vote—Republican, Democratic, and splinter parties. Each national table is followed by a brief listing of the candidates and their national vote with an identification of the characteristics of the state vote. Special aspects of the Electoral College vote are included, and any variations between the plurality figures in these national tables and the Republican-Democratic plurality figures in the state sections are listed. Each state data section is followed by notes giving a detailed composition of the vote and indicating any special circumstances of the state vote—canvassing problems, organization of new counties, dual elector tickets, and so forth.

The major sources for the first volume of this collection are the two pioneer research studies of Edgar Eugene Robinson, *The Presidential Vote,* 1896-1932 (Stanford, Calif.: Stanford University Press, 1934) and *They Voted For Roosevelt: The Presidential Vote,* 1932-1944 (Stanford, Calif.: Stanford University Press, 1947).

Book of the States. Lexington, Ky.: Council of State Governments, 1970–71—.
(Annotated in Chapter 4e.)

The Book of World Rankings. George Thomas Kurian. New York: Facts on File, 1979.
Americans commonly proclaim that the United States is the greatest country in the world. Useful for both the curious and the disputatious, this source book ranks the countries of the world on 326 indicators ranging from total land area data to sugar consumption.

The British Voter: An Atlas and Survey Since 1885. Michael Kinnear. New York: St. Martin's Press, 1981 (c1968).
This is a second edition of a 1968 volume consisting of maps and statistical data on general election results beginning in 1855 and ending in 1979. It also contains brief commentaries on each election.

Canada Votes: A Handbook of Federal and Provincial Election Data. Howard A. Scarrow. New Orleans: Hauser Press, 1962.
Contains relatively complete election results for the period covered, in addition to descriptive essays on Canadian politics.

Compendium of Social Statistics. New York: United Nations, 1963—.
A yearly compendium containing statistics that show the conditions of life and work in the nations of the world, infant mortality, dwelling size, expenditure levels, labor force, and conditions of employment.

Congressional Quarterly's Guide to U.S. Elections. Washington, D.C.: Congressional Quarterly, Inc., 1975.
(Annotated in Chapter 3f.)

Convention Decision and Voting Records. 2d ed. Richard C. Bain and Judith H. Parris. Washington, D.C.: Brookings Institution, 1973.
Analyzes each political convention from 1832 to the early 1970s (organization, rules, factions, votes), and then relates convention behavior to the respective formal elections.

County and City Data Book. U.S. Bureau of Census. Washington, D.C.: Government Printing Office, 1952—.
(Annotated in Chapter 4e.)

A Cross Polity Survey. Arthur S. Banks and Robert Textor. Cambridge, Mass.: MIT Press, 1968.
A basic source of both data in comparative politics and the methodology for using them. The bulk of the work consists of carefully edited computer printouts in sentence form covering a broad range of social, economic, and

political data on every independent nation in the world. The data, along with the contextual explorations, are useful for research on a large number of topics.

Data Bases, Computers, and the Social Sciences. Ralph Bisco, ed. New York: Wiley-Interscience, 1970.

Coordinates the projects of nearly every data archive in the United States and Canada. It distributes to members information on the accessibility of particular survey data in the U.S. and abroad. The CSSDA invites queries from students regarding the location of data in the social sciences.

Deadline Data on World Affairs. Greenwich, Conn.: Deadline Data, 1956—.

Published four times a month on 5" x 8" cards, the data are arranged alphabetically by country and subfiled under "general," "domestic," or "foreign policy" categories. Occasionally something is filed by subject, such as "selective service." Since 1968 a monthly compilation of these data has been published under the title *On Record.* This is an especially useful source for a quick summary or chronology of a recent political event.

Demographic Yearbook. Statistical Office. New York: United Nations, 1948—.

(Annotated in Chapter 2c.)

Directory of Data Bases in the Social and Behavioral Sciences. Vivian S. Sessions, ed. New York. Published in cooperation with the City University of New York by Science Associates International, 1974.

Today, most colleges have a computer facility, and many political science professors have an interest in class research projects utilizing computer-based data. For either purpose, this directory is invaluable because it lists hundreds of sources of computer-based data, stating the nature of the data, their form, how they were obtained, and how the researcher may obtain them.

Directory of Federal Statistics for Local Areas: A Guide to Sources. Urban Update 1977–1978. John D. McCall, ed. Washington, D.C.: Dept. of Commerce, U.S. Bureau of Census, 1980.

(Annotated in Chapter 4e.)

Encyclopedia of the Third World. 2 vols. George Thomas Kurian. New York: Facts on File, 1979.

(Annotated in Chapter 3k.)

Facts on File: Weekly World News Digest with Cumulative Index. New York: Facts on File, Inc., 1940—.

(Annotated in Chapter 3g.)

1976 Federal Campaign Finances. Washington: Common Cause, 1977. Formerly titled *1972 Federal Campaign Finances, Interest Groups and Political Parties*. Washington, D.C.: Common Cause, 1973.

The raw data of political finance are found in this book—who received how much from whom. There are only a few pages of interpretation but several volumes of facts. These data are extensive enough to correlate with voting records or any other behavioral indicators. A rich source.

Guide to Resources and Services: 1981–1982. Inter-University Consortium for Political and Social Research. Ann Arbor, Mich.: The Center of Political Studies, The Institute for Social Research, The University of Michigan, 1982—.

The Inter-University Consortium for Political and Social Research (ICPSR) serves as an archive for machine-readable data on social phenomena for over 130 countries. This annual guide contains a subject index and a principal investigative index with each entry annotated to provide the reader with a ready ability to determine whether a particular data set may be useful. Colleges and universities that are members of the Consortium may order data sets from this *Guide*.

There are other data archive centers in the United States and in other countries. Many have listings of their own holdings. By writing these centers you can obtain listings of their holdings. We have listed the addresses of a few of the better known centers.

Data & Program Library Service
4451 Social Science Building
University of Wisconsin
Madison, Wisconsin 53706

National Opinion Research Center
University of Chicago
6030 South Ellis Avenue
Chicago, Illinois 60637

Roper Public Opinion Research Center
University of Connecticut
Storrs, Connecticut 06268

Guide to U.S. Government Statistics. 4th ed. John L. Andriot. McLean, Va.: Documents Index, 1973—.

Indexes federal statistical sources by subject and outlines the statistical output of each agency.

The International Almanac of Electoral History. Thomas Mackie and Richard Rose. New York: Facts on File, 1982.

Formerly listed under the same title and authors, but published in London: Macmillan, 1974.

Scores of Western nations have held contested elections since World War II. This source supplies a brief chapter on the political history of each of these countries, and is especially useful for comparative data because of the standard format.

International Guide to Electoral Statistics. Stein Rokkan and Jean Meyriat, eds. The Hague: Morton, 1969.

A series of elaborate essays describing how to locate election data in 14 European countries. It also includes detailed historical material on the electoral process in each country.

National Basic Intelligence Factbook. U.S. Central Intelligence Agency. Washington, D.C. Government Printing Office, 1979.

Contains basic information on most of the nations of the world. Arranged alphabetically by country it presents such information as population size, ethnic divisions, religion, language, literacy rate, size of the labor force, political system, and economic data. It is superseded from time to time with new issuances.

SETUPS: American Politics (Supplementary Empirical Teaching Units in Political Science). The Inter-University Consortium for Political Research Through an Agreement with the American Political Science Association. Washington, D.C.: American Political Science Association, 1975—.

Data collected by subject specialists are made available to students and scholars on a variety of topics. The data are placed in accessible format so that students may learn how to analyze data as well as to gain an appreciation for the substantive materials of a course. Each data SETUP is accompanied by a brief book containing exercises, data codebooks, and bibliography. Instructors will determine whether a particular SETUP is computer ready and thus accessible at the institution. The following SETUPS are available:

Voting Behavior: The 1976 Election by Bruce D. Bowen, C. Anthony Broh, Charles L. Prysby.

Political Socialization Across the Generations by Paul Allen Beck, Jere W. Bruner, L. Douglas Dobson.

Political Participation by F. Christopher Arterton, Harlan Hahn.

Representation in the United States Congress: 1973 by Ray A. Geigle, Peter G. Hartjens.

The Supreme Court in American Politics: Policy Through Law by John Paul Ryan, C. Neal Tate.

The Dynamics of Political Budgeting: A Public Policy Simulation by Martin K. Hoffman.

The Fear of Crime by Wesley G. Skogan and William R. Klecka.

SETUPS: Cross-National and World Politics (Supplementary Empirical Teaching Units in Political Science). The Inter-University Consortium for Political

Research Through an Agreement with the American Political Science Association. Washington, D.C.: American Political Science Association, 1977—.

These SETUPS are computer related instructional materials whereby students may be exposed to important substantive topics in cross-national and world politics settings. The following SETUPS are currently available with additional ones in the planning stage.

Comparative Voting Behavior by Herbet B. Asher and Bradley Richardson.

Comparative Budgeting: Policy and Processes by John Creighton Campbell and John M. Echols.

Are Political Values Really Changing? by Charles Lewis Taylor.

Comparing Political Parties by Robert Harmel with Kenneth Janda.

Political Parties of the World. Alan J. Day and Henry W. Degenhardt, eds. Detroit; Gale Research Co., 1980.

Presents factual data on all of the world's active political parties. Fills a significant gap in the literature.

Presidential Ballots, 1836-1892. W. Dean Burnham. Baltimore: Johns Hopkins Press, 1955. Reprinted, New York: Arno Press, 1976.

In addition to exhaustive data, this book includes incisive essays on party politics during the era of sectionalism.

Social Indicators. Washington, D.C.: Office of Management and Budget and U.S. Department of Commerce, 1973—.

(Annotated in Chapter 4c.)

Source Books of American Presidential Campaign and Election Statistics, 1948-1968. John H. Runyon, Jennefer Verdini, and Sally S. Runyon. New York: F. Ungar, 1971.

One might think that the data on electing the President would be readily available, but they are seldom compiled in a usable form. The campaign itineraries, for example, are seldom as easily available as in this work. It also has considerable data on media exposure and cost, campaign staffs, voting in preference primaries, etc. . . .

The Statesman's Year Book: Statistical and Historical Annual of the States of the World. New York: St. Martin's Press, 1864—.

Exhaustive compilation of statistics and descriptions of various countries A to Z. Included is history, area and population, constitution, defense economy, natural resources, industry, trade, communications, religion, education and diplomatic representation. Also includes a short section at the end of each country description titled "Books of Reference."

Statistical Abstract for Latin America. Center of Latin American Studies. Los Angeles: University of California, 1955—.

This annually issued volume presents current statistical data on all Latin American nations and their dependencies. Information is offered on area, population, social organization, economic characteristics, finances, foreign trade, and other special topics. Notes and source information accompany its tables; it contains a bibliography.

A Statistical History of the American Presidential Elections, with Supplementary Tables Covering 1968-1980. Svend Petersen. Westport, Conn.: Greenwood Press, 1981.

Formerly titled *A Statistical History of the American Presidential Elections.* (Svend Petersen. New York: Ungar, 1963). A useful compilation, this volume contains complete statistics on American presidential elections, with tables for each of the 50 states and each of the 11 historical parties.

The Statistical History of the United States, From Colonial Times to the Present. New York: Basic Books, 1976.

Supersedes similar information in: *Historical Statistics of the United States, Colonial Times to 1957,* which was published by the Government Printing Office in 1960.

United Nations Statistical Yearbook. New York: United Nations Statistical Office, 1949—.

A continuation of the *Statistical Yearbook of the League of Nations, 1927-1945.* Because of the upheaval of World War II, it was not published between 1945 and 1949. Its tables cover world population, manpower, agriculture, production, mining, construction, consumption, transportation, external trade, wages, prices, national income, finance, social statistics, education, and culture. A 10-to-20-year period is generally given for each series of statistics. It is arranged by subject, has a nation index, and is printed in French and English. Current data for many tables are published regularly by the United Nations Statistical Office in its *Monthly Bulletin of Statistics.*

United Nations World Economic Survey. Department of Economic and Social Affairs. New York: United Nations, 1945-1976.

Yearly charts interpret the economic trends of the world in this survey. This book spawns a supplement of detailed studies of entire continental regions.

United Nations Yearbook of National Accounts Statistics. New York: United Nations Statistical Office and Department of Economic and Social Affairs, 1958—.

Concerned with the gross national product of each nation and generally includes a complete financial picture (government spending and income, consumer consumption, etc.).

World Almanac and Book of Facts. New York: Newspaper Enterprise Association, 1868—.
(Annotated in Chapter 2c.)

World Handbook of Political and Social Indicators. 2d ed., 3rd ed., 1980. Charles Lewis Taylor and Michael C. Hudson. New Haven, Conn.: Yale University Press, 1972.
Many sources containing statistical data are difficult to relate to topics in political science. With this source, however, one can write an original research paper using basic, politically relevant data. For example, the work contains detailed material on political protest and executive change, foreign aid, telephones-per-thousand, riots, ethnic minorities, urbanization, etc. If a student wants to write an exciting *data-based* paper, this is a good but now dated source. Included are essays on interpreting the data, computer programming, and analysis.

Yearbook on International Communist Affairs. Milorad M. Drachkovitch. Stanford, Calif.: Hoover Institute, 1967—.
(Annotated in Chapter 2c.)

Polls

California Poll. San Francisco: Field Institute.
The California electorate is one of the most significant in the nation as a harbinger of trends. This poll, concentrated within the state, tests Californians on the most important issue of a particular time and publishes results 35 to 45 times a year.

Directory of Data Bases in the Social and Behavioral Sciences. Vivian S. Sessions, ed. New York: Published in cooperation with the City University of New York by Science Associates International, 1974.

Gallup Opinion Index. (Formerly *Gallup Political Index*) Princeton, N.J.: Gallup International, 1965—.
Although the Gallup opinion polls are well known and their findings are published regularly in many newspapers, these polls are often neglected by student researchers because of the difficulty of locating a particular poll in an unindexed newspaper. This monthly publication offers an answer to that problem through the publication of monthly surveys covering a wide range of subjects, from the Supreme Court to the "Most Admired Women."

The Gallup Poll: Public Opinion, 1935-1971. Three volumes. George H. Gallup. New York: Random House, 1972.

The Gallup Poll: Public Opinion, 1972-1981. Six volumes. George H. Gallup. Wilmington, Del.: Scholarly Resources Inc., 1978, 1979, 1980, 1981, 1982.

These nine volumes, plus additional ones to be published, contain the public polls conducted by the George Gallup organization. These polls touch upon almost every controversial political and social question since the mid-1930s. Students can use these poll results in supporting their factual claims as to the state of mass public opinion.

The Harris Survey Yearbook of Public Opinion. New York: Louis Harris and Associates, 1971—.

The Harris organization polls cover far more areas than are published in newspapers. The breakdown and subdivision of each question are very detailed in this compendium, which contains useful basis data for research.

Index to International Public Opinion, 1978-79—. Elizabeth Hann Hastings and Philip K. Hastings. Westport, Conn.: Greenwood Press, 1979.

This annual publication brings together public opinion surveys from around the world. Not confined to political science survey research, this index contains market research, corporate relations, and other specific subject surveys.

Minnesota Poll. Otto A. Silha, ed. Minneapolis, Minn.: Minneapolis Star and Tribune, 1964—.

Published in the Sunday editions of the *Minneapolis Tribune;* a 20-year summary was published in 1964 under the title, *Twenty Years of Minnesota Opinion, 1944-1964: Minneapolis Tribune's Minnesota Poll.*

Public Opinion, 1935-1946. Hadley Cantril. Princeton, N.J.: Princeton University Press; reprinted, Westport, Conn.: Greenwood Press, 1978.

A massive collection of public opinion polls during these years. While dated, the topical range is extensive, and the material is useful for comparative purposes.

Public Opinion: Changing Attitudes on Contemporary Political and Social Issues. Robert Chandler. New York: R. R. Bowker, 1972.

Contains polls commissioned by CBS News on the important issues of the late 1960s and early 1970s such as women's rights, marijuana, and the environment. Results are broken down in terms of an interesting set of categories: parents of reform-oriented youth, parents of radical youth, etc. There are extensive comment and analysis.

Roper Public Opinion Poll. Williamstown, Mass.: Williams College.

The most exhaustive file of poll data in existence, this source concentrates on all academic and professional poll and survey groups from around the world. The surveys and studies are available to students on cards or tapes at reasonable rates.

Sourcebook of Harris National Surveys: Repeated Questions 1963-1976. Elizabeth Martin, Diana McDuffe, Stanley Presser. Chapel Hill, N.C.: Institute for Research in Social Science, University of North Carolina, Chapel Hill, 1981.

Matches questionnaire items from more than 400 Harris surveys of diverse populations and subject matters. This volume does not give the survey results. Rather, it shows which Harris polls asked the same or closely similar questions. Once ascertained, these data may be requested from the Louis Harris Data Center at the University of North Carolina at Chapel Hill. Thus, researchers can analyze social change based on surveys conducted between 1967 and 1976; some studies date since 1963.

4b Quantitative Applications

There are a number of fine statistics books written for both general social science and political science audiences. We will not attempt to list all the titles here. Instructors will no doubt lead their students to what they believe are the best currently available texts. However, we will annotate a few of the widely employed statistical packages and draw attention to a number of useful methodological works which emphasize statistical tools.

Applied Factor Analysis. Rudolph J. Rummel. Evanston, Ill.: Northwestern University Press, 1970.

This is a lengthy and in-depth treatment of a particular statistical method which is employed to determine underlying dimensions of variables actually measured through the rotation of correlation matrices.

BMDP Statistical Software 1981. W. J. Dixon, ed. Berkeley, Calif.: University of California Press, 1981.

This particular statistical package first appeared in 1961 and was for many political scientists the first introduction to "canned" programs. Since those early days this package has been expanded from biomedical applications to almost every aspect of social science statistical technique. Also see *SPSS^x User's Guide* and *SAS User's Guide* in this section.

Content Analysis for the Social Sciences and Humanities. Ole Holsti. Reading, Mass.: Addison-Wesley, 1969.

Content analysis entails any number of methods employed to analyze various forms of verbal communication such as government documents, political speeches, and news stories. This book examines the theory and practice of content analysis with illustrations.

Empirical Political Analysis: Research Methods in Political Science. Jarol B. Manheim and Richard C. Rich. Englewood Cliffs, N.J.: Prentice-Hall, Inc., 1981.

One of a number of texts that treat all aspects of empirical political research. Describes techniques and provides examples which political science students will find useful and familiar.

Evaluation: A Systematic Approach. Peter Rossi. Beverly Hills, Calif.: Sage Publications, 1979.

Political scientists are sometimes asked to assess how particular policy choices have worked out. For example, does the death penalty really deter murder? Obviously such research is difficult to conduct. This particular book, comprehensive in scope, provides many examples of the process and difficulties encountered in evaluation research.

Experimental and Quasi-Experimental Designs for Research. Donald Campbell and Julian Stanley. Chicago: Rand McNally, 1963.

While experimentation in political science is difficult to execute, more and more studies are employing such techniques. Additionally, political scientists have attempted to approximate experimental design by controlling as much as the potential bias as possible in what is known as quasi-experimental research designs. This book explains the logic and methods of experimentation in social science research.

Handbook of Research Design and Social Measurement. 3rd ed. Delbert C. Miller. New York: David McKay Company, Inc., 1977.

An excellent guide to research design and sampling, data collection, statistical analysis, sociometric scales or index selection, research funding, costing, and reporting. Very helpful to both novice and accomplished researchers.

An Introduction to Political Science Methods. Robert A. Bernstein and James A. Dyer. Englewood Cliffs, N.J.: Prentice-Hall, Inc., 1979.

This beginning text covers hypotheses formulation, explanation, measurement, sample procedures, data collection and sources, correlational analysis, tests of significance, and regression techniques. It contains exercises and a fine glossary of technical terms.

Introduction to the Use of Computer Packages for Statistical Analyses. Richard Morre. Englewood Cliffs, N.J.: Prentice-Hall, 1978.

A primer on how to use the computer. It provides basic information useful for operating three widely used computer packages—SAS, SPSS, and BMD.

Issues and Parties in Legislative Voting: Methods of Statistical Analysis. Duncan MacRae, Jr. New York: Harper and Row, Publishers, 1970.

Focuses upon roll-call voting and applies a variety of statistical techniques to explore how rigorous analysis may be applied to describing and explaining legislative coalitions.

The Practice of Social Research. 3rd ed. Earl Babbie. Belmont, Calif.: Wadsworth Publishing Co., 1983.

A first rate text introducing research methods in the social sciences. Covers such topics as "human inquiry and science," "conceptualization and measurement," "indexes, scales, and typologies," and "the ethics and politics of social research."

Quantitative Applications in the Social Sciences: A Sage University Paper Series. Beverly Hills, Calif.: Sage Publications, 1976—.

Below is a list of currently available monographs which provide readers with limited mathematical backgrounds explanations and demonstrations of various statistical techniques applicable to political science data. Most will find these titles very helpful.

Analysis of Variance by Gudmund R. Iversen and Helmut Norpoth

Operations Research Methods by Stuart Nagel with Marian Neef

Causal Modeling by Herbert B. Asher

Tests of Significance by Ramon E. Henkel

Cohort Analysis by Norval D. Glenn

Canonical Analysis and Factor Comparison by Mark S. Levine

Analysis of Nominal Data by H. T. Reynolds

Analysis of Ordinal Data by David K. Hildebrand, James D. Laing, and Howard Rosenthal

Time Series Analysis: Regression Techniques by Charles W. Ostrom, Jr.

Ecological Inference by Laura Irwin Langbein and Allan J. Lichtman

Multidimensional Scaling by Joseph B. Kruskal and Myron Wish

Analysis of Covariance by Albert R. Wildt and Olli Ahtola

Introduction to Factor Analysis by Jae-On Kim and Charles W. Mueller

Factor Analysis by Jae-On Kim and Charles W. Mueller

Multiple Indicators: An Introduction by John L. Sullivan and Stanley Feldman

Exploratory Data Analysis by Frederick Hartwig with Brian E. Dearing

Reliability and Validity Assessment by Edward G. Carmines and Richard A. Zeller

Analyzing Panel Data by Gregory B. Markus

Discriminant Analysis by William R. Klecka

Log-Linear Models by David Knoke and Peter J. Burke

Interrupted Time Series Analysis by David McDowall, Richard McCleary, Errol E. Meidinger, and Richard A. Hay, Jr.

Applied Regression: An Introduction by Michael S. Lewis-Beck

Research Designs by Paul E. Spector

Unidimensional Scaling by John P. McIver and Edward G. Carmines

Magnitude Scaling by Milton Lodge

Multiattribute Analysis by Ward Edwards and J. Robert Newman

Dynamic Modeling: An Introduction by R. Robert Huckfeldt, C. W. Kohfeld, and Thomas W. Likens

Network Analysis by David Knoke and James H. Kuklinski

Interpreting and Using Regression by Christopher H. Achen

Quantitative Analysis of Judicial Behavior. Glendon A. Schubert. Glencoe, Ill.: The Free Press and the Bureau of Social and Political Research, Michigan State University, 1959.

A somewhat dated but still useful book for judicial scholars. It analyzes and illustrates through real examples how to use bloc analysis, game analysis, and scalogram analysis in describing and explaining judicial decision making.

Quantitative Methods for Public Administration: Techniques and Applications. Susan Welch and John C. Comer. Homewood, Ill.: Dorsey Press, 1983.

Targeted at students training to do research in public policy and administration, this book concentrates on the application of statistical tools and quantitative techniques. Traditional areas of concern such as descriptive statistics and multiple regression are supplemented with subject relevant topics such as cost-benefit analysis and quantitative techniques for planning.

Questionnaire Design and Attitude Measurement. A. N. Oppenheim. New York: Basic Books, 1966.

A complete treatment of the theory and construction of questionnaires.

SAS User's Guide: 1979 Edition. SAS Institute. Cary, N.C., 1979.

SAS contains a variety of "canned" computer programs useful to students of political science. In its earlier editions SAS tended to concentrate on ratio or interval level statistical program. However, this edition contains a variety of programs applicable to nominal and ordinal data. Many colleges and universities possess both SAS and SPSS (below). Both packages are easy to use.

Social Statistics. 2d rev. ed. Hubert Blalock, Jr. New York: McGraw-Hill, 1979.

One of the best known and widely adopted textbooks on statistics for the social sciences. Author introduces all types of statistics; the book is very good on multivariate statistics including recently adopted techniques such as log-linear analysis.

SPSS^x User's Guide. SPSS Inc. New York: McGraw-Hill Book Co., 1983.

SPSS is the most common social science statistical package available. It discusses and illustrates how to use this integrated system of computer programs which is tailor-made for social science students. It also discusses the meaning of a variety of the statistics contained in this package. Occasional updates are published.

Statistics and Public Policy. William B. Fairley and Frederick Mosteller, eds. Reading, Mass.: Addison-Wesley Publishing Co., 1977.

This volume contains articles which illustrate the application of statistics to public policy. Students with limited backgrounds in mathematics will find the examples useful in understanding the circumstances when statistics are useful to the policy analyst.

Survey Sampling. Leslie Kish. New York: John Wiley and Sons, 1965.
Considered the definitive statement on survey sampling. It is a very exhaustive treatment which covers practically every aspect of this common political science technique.

GOVERNMENT DOCUMENTS AND RELATED MATERIALS

A government document is any publication issued by a governmental body at public expense. We have also included in this section publications about governmental bodies which are not necessarily government publications but nonetheless bear a close content relation. Government documents are a rich source of information and data about government and politics. These sources have been relatively neglected during the last several decades due in part to the professional enchantment with survey research. However, government agencies keep records, make reports, issue rules and regulations and, generally speaking, create paper trails. These trails contain helpful signposts for traversing research terrain.

The fact is that government documents possess huge amounts of basic information at no or very low cost while survey research has become increasingly expensive. Discover the documents section of your college library. It contains an amazing amount of useful information. In many cases it may be a bit confusing the first time one tries to use a government document, as the information tends to be organized according to the structure of the issuing agency. For this reason, we have included several key guides to the use of government documents.

4c U.S. National and International Documents

American Foreign Policy: Current Documents. Historical Office of the Bureau of Public Affairs. Washington, D.C.: Government Printing Office, 1941—.
A yearly publication that gathers the more important messages, declarations, treaties, and so forth, that have surfaced during the year.

American Statistics Index. Washington, D.C.: Congressional Information Service, 1973—.
(Annotated Chapter 2f.)

Congressional Information Service Index to Publications of the United States Congress. Washington, D.C., 1970—.
(Annotated in Chapter 4d.)

The Constitution and What It Means Today. 14th ed. Edward Samuel Corwin. Revised by Harold W. Chase and Craig R. Ducat. Princeton, N.J.: Princeton University Press, 1978.

A definitive work on the United States Constitution. Article by article, amendment by amendment, this authoritative work summarizes the leading legal cases that have shaped the interpretation of the Constitution. For example, the precise definition of the "right to a speedy and public trial," may be found in this book, followed by a concise summary of applicable cases.

Corwin and Peltason's Understanding the Constitution. 8th ed. J. W. Peltason. New York: Holt, Rinehart and Winston, 1979.
A nontechnical discussion of the main features of the U.S. Constitution and its historical and practical significance as applied today.

Directory of Information Resources in the United States. The National Referral Center for Science and Technology of the Library of Congress. Washington, D.C.: Government Printing Office, published irregularly.
To obtain material from this source, it is necessary to know precisely what one wants. This directory contains what librarians term "fugitive material," items that are available to the public on request only, and when the supply is exhausted it is unobtainable. This guide supplies a list of most federal and federally sponsored agencies (such as the East-West Center of the University of Hawaii), and describes their activities and the type of data available from each. Most of the material comes in the form of printed government documents and in typewritten and mimeographed reports. Also see *Directory of Information and Referral Services in the U.S. and Canada.* 2d ed. Corazon Estene-Doyle, ed. Phoenix, Ariz.: Alliance of Information Services, 1978—.

Everyman's United Nations. 9th ed. New York: United Nations Department of Public Information, 1979—.
The primary source for the structure, functions, and work of the United Nations and its related agencies. A frequently revised handbook, it is broken into four parts. Part 1 discusses the organization of the United Nations; Part 2 is concerned with political, social, economic, and security questions; Part 3, specialized agencies, such as the Food and Agriculture Organization (FAO), the United Nations Educational, Scientific, and Cultural Organization (UNESCO), and many others; Part 4 an index, the chronology, and a list of the United Nations Information Centers.

Federal Career Directory: A Guide for College Students. United States Civil Service Commission. Washington, D.C.: Government Printing Office, 1956—.
This is one of a dozen or so guides to federal employment. The commission's regional offices also publish separate local guides.

Federal Register. Washington, D.C.: Government Printing Office, 1936—.
Published five times a week, the *Federal Register* includes presidential executive orders, proclamations, reorganization plans, and rules and regula-

tions issued by executive departments and agencies. It is accurate and complete.

Foreign Relations of the U.S.: Diplomatic Papers. Department of State. Washington, D.C.: Government Printing Office, 1862—.
   (Annotated in Chapter 3f.)

Guide to U.S. Government Statistics. 4th ed. John L. Andriot. McLean, Va.: Documents Index, 1973—.
   (Annotated in Chapter 4a.)

Guide to the United Nations Organization Documentation and Publishing for Students, Researchers, Librarians. Peter I. Hajnal. Oceana, 1978.
   This publication supplies the researcher with an exhaustive description of the documents classification system, a list of the many UN publications, and various approaches to research projects in general.

Guide to American Foreign Relations Since 1700. Edited by Richard Dean Burns. ABC CLIO, Inc. Santa Barbara, California, 1983.
   This guide is both thorough and very helpfully organized. A beginning chapter, covering surveys, themes and theories, is an excellent first stop in searching for a topic in the area of U.S. foreign relations. The remaining chapters cover the field both chronologically and topically. Chronological chapters thoroughly cover the history of U.S. foreign policy. Topical chapters focus on U.S. relations with various countries, such as the Soviet Union, economic issues, international organization and military policy.

A Guide to Federal Consumer Services. Washington, D.C.: Dept. of Health and Human Services, Office of Consumer Affairs, 1976—.
   Over 50 government agencies provide services to the consumer. This guide outlines the major purpose and function, legal background of each program, how the law is enforced, and how one contacts the appropriate agency to get help.

Housing and Planning References. Department of Housing and Urban Development. Washington, D.C.: Government Printing Office, 1948—.
   This bimonthly publication selects key books and articles in a variety of politically related areas such as zoning, pollution, crime and law enforcement, noise control, and low-income housing.

Freedom of Information Guide. Want Publishing Company. Washington, D.C.
   (Annotated in Chapter 3b.)

Introduction to United States Public Documents. 2d ed. Joe Mosehead. Littleton, Colo.: Libraries Unlimited Inc., 1978.

Surveys documents and describes how they are organized and available. This is the most thorough guide to U.S. documents presently available. While it is not light reading, it is direct and factual. Reading the appropriate section helps to focus the research and to forge questions for librarians.

Nomination and Election of the President and Vice President of the United States, Including the Manner of Selecting Delegates to National Political Conventions. Compiled by Thomas M. Durbin and Michael V. Seitzinger for the U. S. Senate Library. Washington, D.C.: Government Printing Office, 1980.

Presidential selection is a complex process involving primaries, state conventions, state party rules, and a multitude of national and state laws. This is the most usable compilation of these data, revised frequently.

Popular Names of U.S. Government Reports: A Catalogue. 3rd ed. Bernard A. Bernier, Jr., Katherine F. Gould, Porter Humphrey. Washington, D.C.: Government Printing Office, 1976.

Although many significant reports are popularly known by the name of one of the responsible officials, such popular names are seldom part of the official title. From a clue so slim as, say, "The Kerner Report," this guide can lead to the exact citation.

Public Affairs Information Service Bulletin. Robert S. Wilson, ed. New York: Public Affairs Information Service, 1915—.

(Annotated in Chapter 2f.)

Shepard's Acts and Cases by Popular Names—Federal and State. 2d ed. Colorado Springs: Shepards, Inc. 1968—.

Many important laws are cited by popular names (i.e., the Homestead Act), but to read the law the proper legal citation is needed. This source answers such questions.

Statistical Abstract of the United States. Bureau of Census. Washington, D.C.: Governmental Printing Office, 1879—.

Published annually, this is a recognized, reliable summary of statistics on the social, political, and economic organization of the United States. It also serves as a guide to other statistical publications and sources through the introductory text to each section, the source notes for each table, and the bibliography of sources. Here one may find information of primarily national concern. Also included, however, are many tables for regions and individual states and statistics for the Commonwealth of Puerto Rico and other outlying areas of the United States.

Additional information for cities, counties, metropolitan areas, congressional districts, and other small units is available in supplements to the *Statistical Abstract* (such as *County and City Data Book; Congressional District Data Book; Historical Statistics of the U.S., Colonial Times to 1957, Continuation to 1962 and Revisions*). *The Statistical Abstract* is the most reliable source for such data as births, deaths, marriages, and divorces; number of physicians, dentists, and nurses; immigration and naturalization; law enforcement, courts, and prisons; geography and climate; public lands and parks; recreation and travel; elections; and incomes.

The Statistical History of the United States, From Colonial Times to the Present. New York: Basic Books, 1976.

This work supersedes similar information in *Historical Statistics of the United States, Colonial Times to 1957*, which was published by the Government Printing Office in 1960. It is a supplement to the *Statistical Abstract of the United States*, which contains more than 8,000 statistical studies grouped mostly into yearly periods. It covers economic and social development from 1610 to 1957 and includes definitions of terms and descriptive text. Source notes provide a guide for students who wish to read the original published sources for further reference and data. It contains a complete subject index alphabetically arranged.

Social Indicators. Washington, D.C.: Office of Management and Budget and U.S. Department of Commerce, 1973—.

This irregularly issued publication groups data around major significant goals—good health, long life, fear of crime, etc. The status of the population is then measured against major social indicators. The focus is on the end products (not the institutions delivering the services) and on actual educational attainment rather than on school budgets. Each topic includes a brief essay as well as colorful, concise, easy-to-read charts and graphs. This is clearly a first stop if one is interested in a major problem. Published triennially, there are also volumes for 1976 and 1980.

Subject Guide to Major U.S. Government Publications. Ellen Pauline Jackson. Chicago: American Library Association, 1968.

Because the official guides index government publications under the name of the issuing agency, which may not be known to the researcher, few students, on starting their inquiries, can identify the important government publications relevant to their topic. This guide gives an annotated bibliography of key government documents on general topics, such as "nuclear disarmament" as well as suggested cross references.

Synopsis of United Nations Cases in the Field of Peace and Security 1946-67. Catherine Teng. New York: Taplinger, 1968.

A short work that presents one-page summaries of each action. In an area where many documents are extremely lengthy, this is a valuable compilation. It is arranged by nation with an appendix on international conflict.

United Nations World Economic Survey. Department of Economic and Social Affairs. New York: United Nations, 1945–1976.
(Annotated in Chapter 4a.)

UNDOC Current Index. New York: United Nations, 1950—.
(Annotated in Chapter 2f.)

United States Code and United States Statutes At Large. Washington, D.C.: Government Printing Office, 1875—.
(Annotated in Chapter 4d.)

United Nations Statistical Yearbook. New York: United Nations Statistical Office, 1949—.
(Annotated in Chapter 4a.)

United States Government Manual (1935-73). Washington, D.C.: Office of the Federal Register, 1974—.
This is the official organization manual of the United States Government. It describes the purpose and programs of most of its agencies and lists top personnel. It is the first basic source for information on the federal bureaucracy.

United States Reports. Washington, D.C.: Government Printing Office, 1790—.
This is a yearly compilation of each decision rendered by the United States Supreme Court. Most decisions include majority, dissenting, and concurring opinions. These opinions contain the sweep of facts, attitudes, and legal concepts relating to the important issues that come before the Supreme Court.

U.S. Senate Factual Campaign Information. Washington, D.C.: Government Printing Office, 1978.
Originally for use by senators in their own re-election campaigns, this is a compilation of state primary laws, previous votes, and relevant administrative and Senate rulings.

United States Treaties and Other International Agreements. U.S. Department of State. Washington, D.C.: Government Printing Office, 1950—.
Formerly titled *United States Treaties and Other International Acts,* this is a series of publications listing all treaties and agreements to which the United States has become a party during a specific year.

Weekly Compilation of Presidential Documents. Washington, D.C.: Government Printing Office, 1965—.

Published every Monday under the auspices of the Office of the Federal Register, National Archives and Records Service, and General Services Administration, this source contains the presidential materials released by the White House up to 5 p.m., eastern time, the preceding Friday. It includes the President's addresses, remarks, announcements, appointments and nominations, executive orders, memoranda, meetings with foreign leaders, and proclamations, as well as reports to the President.

World Strength of Communist Party Organizations. Department of State, Bureau of Intelligence and Research. Washington, D.C.: Government Printing Office, 1970.

Here are detailed, readable reports of communist activity in many countries. The reports describe the source of communist strength, elected officials, election results, etc.

4d Congressional Documents

One can use the basic documents of Congress as primary data sources, provided one has some background on the issue being studied (which can be gained from the *Congressional Quarterly Weekly Report, see Chapter 3g*) and is not smothered by the massive output of legislative documents. In the following pages, the basic legislative documents necessary for a term paper are described. Most are available in a government depository library, of which there are over a thousand throughout the United States. Some, such as the *Congressional Record,* are available in almost any college library. A few, such as current bills, can be obtained from any member of Congress. In this instance, be sure to allow enough time (at least ten days) to receive the bills. The basic documents described herein are the following:

1. *Congressional Record*
2. House and Senate journals
3. House, Senate, and conference reports
4. Proceedings of hearings
5. Bills and the digest of public bills
6. *Calendars of the United States House of Representatives and History of Legislation*
7. *Congressional Serial Set*
8. Other basic congressional documents

Note the bibliographic citations in Chapter 5 for the correct way to cite or request a bill or a hearing report.

CONGRESSIONAL RECORD. Washington, D.C.: Government Printing Office, 1873—. The *Record* is a nearly verbatim account of everything uttered aloud on the floor of Congress as well as of some material not actually spoken but entered as an "extension of remarks." It is published Monday through Friday while Congress is in session. It is a valuable source also because legislators frequently insert letters and articles that are in themselves primary sources of information on topics under discussion.

Before 1873 the *Congressional Record* was titled *Congressional Globe* (1833–1873); before that it was called *The Register of Debates* (1824–1837); and even earlier, *Annals of Congress* (1789–1824). It is cataloged under these titles in libraries. Each set consists of 15 to 20 parts a year, including a separate index. In 1947 the *Daily Digest* volumes were added, which review highlights, list scheduled hearings of Congress, and summarize day-to-day committee activity.

The *Congressional Record* contains a two-part index, consisting of an alphabetical listing of subjects and names and a history of bills and resolutions arranged by their numbers. This second section is considered the best available source for tracing the route of a particular bill. Because this is a daily record, the best method of locating information is first to establish the date on which the debate took place.

A student may request to be placed on the mailing list for the *Congressional Record*. It is a free service rendered by legislators to their constituents. However, unless the student is willing to read and digest some 200 pages a day, this would be wasteful, as each legislator is limited to a relatively small number of such free subscriptions.

HOUSE AND SENATE JOURNALS. These two separate documents are published by each house at the end of a session. They are essentially official, trimmed-down versions of the *Congressional Record*, with debates and all other matters excluded. Included are motions, votes, and actions taken.

HOUSE, SENATE, AND CONFERENCE REPORTS. These are the reports of the committee of Congress dealing with a particular measure. They include data on the actual suggested legislation to be sent to the floor and the majority, minority, and concurring reports, which usually outline the issues around the measure. Especially interesting are reports from conferences, which involve both House and Senate members. When read with an understanding of the context of a measure, which one can gain from the *Congressional Quarterly*, these reports can form the backbone of an original research paper.

PROCEEDINGS OF HEARINGS. Congressional hearings are an incredibly rich source of material, but it must be used intelligently. Appropriations hearings are particularly good. For the results of digging through the proceedings of such hearings, see Aaron Wildavsky, *The Politics of the Budgetary Process* (Boston: Little, Brown, 1973), and Albert P. Melone, *Lawyers, Public Policy and Interest Group Politics* (Washington, D.C.: University Press of America, 1977).

The bulk of hearings reports is enormous because legislators frequently do not wish to listen to long, detailed expositions and simply say, "Just insert your presentation in the record." Thus, the proceedings of a hearing often contain reprints of all the essential material relevant to a particular issue. These reports are available selectively in depository libraries, from the Government Printing Office (for a fee), and sometimes *free* from the chairperson of a commmittee *while the hearings are in progress or until the initial supply is exhausted.*

To obtain hearings reports, it is important to cite them correctly. The citation should include:

1. U.S. Congress
2. The part of Congress (Senate or House)
3. The subcommittee (if any)
4. The committee
5. The title of the hearing
6. The number of the Congress (93rd, 94th, etc.)
7. The session

See the example on page 128.

The sources for identifying current hearings are the following:

Congressional Information Service Index to Publications of the United States Congress. Washington, D.C., 1970—.

Congressional documents contain extensive information on almost every important area of public policy. Without some sort of in-depth index, such as this publication, these reports would be lost to the researcher.

The *CIS Index* analyzes the hundreds of congressional hearing reports and other documents published each year, indexing them by subject so that the researcher can readily identify committee members, witnesses, etc. Moreover, it offers a summary of each document.

The Monthly Catalog of United States Government Publication lists each volume as it is sent to the depository libraries, and is itself sent to each library as an index. These "depository libraries" are usually located at the state universities in the larger cities of every state.

The sources for identifying past hearings (before the publication of *Congressional Information Service Index to Publication of the United States Congress,* above) are: 1) *Cumulative Index of Congressional Committee Hearings (Not Confidential in Character) Second Quadrennial Supplement from the Eighty-Eighth Congress (January 3, 1963) through the Eighty-Ninth Congress (January 3, 1967) together with Committee Prints in the United States Senate Library.* Compiled by Carmen Carpenter under the direction of F. R. Valeo. Washington, D.C.: Government Printing Office, 1967. 2) *Cumulative Index of Congressional Committee Hearings (Not Confidential in Character) Third*

Quadrennial Supplement from the Ninetieth Congress (January 10, 1967) through the Ninety-First Congress (January 2, 1971) together with Selected Committee Prints in the United States Senate Library. Compiled by Carmen Carpenter and Polly Sargent under the direction of F. R. Valeo. Washington, D.C.: Government Printing Office, 1971.

BILLS OF CONGRESS. Before a law is enacted, it is called a bill. Bills can be primary data for one studying the legislative process. They come with the following designations:

H.R. (bill from the House of Representatives)

S. (bill from the Senate)

H. Res. or S. Res. (House resolution or Senate resolution)

H.J. Res. or S.J. Res. (Joint resolutions, depending upon origin)

H. Con. Res. or S. Con. Res. (Concurrent resolutions, depending upon origin)

Digest of Public General Bills and Selected Resolutions with Index. Washington, D.C.: Government Printing Office, 1936—.

Designated by congressional session and issue number, this digest is the legislative product of a session of Congress. It is especially valuable because it includes a digest and legislative history of each measure receiving action, the date reported, the report number, the date of debate, etc. With this information, one can read the debate on the measure in the *Congressional Record,* check the vote, etc. This digest also contains an author or sponsor index so one can see what bills a particular member introduced, and a subject matter index.

CALENDARS OF THE UNITED STATES HOUSE OF REPRESENTATIVES AND HISTORY OF LEGISLATION. These are published daily during each session with a cumulative volume at the end of the session. For the House (the Senate has a calendar, but it is much less elaborate), the calendar is the daily plan of work. On Monday it contains a cumulative legislative history of each pending bill and a subject matter index on pending legislation. It is a status report made during the session, i.e., what is being considered and where, when, and how.

CONGRESSIONAL SERIAL SET. Washington, D.C.: Government Printing Office, 1817—. This set of over 13,500 volumes is a collection of the above mentioned documents, containing House and Senate journals, documents, and reports. It does not include bills, hearings, laws, or "committee prints." The reports are committee reports and are especially important because they contain not only brief summaries of the hearings but also the individual views of the committee members who participated. Committee reports usually contain the best brief summary of all the important facts and arguments concerning the bill in question.

Obviously, it can be difficult to trace a document through such a large number of volumes, so the following indexes, all published by the Government Printing Office, can lead to a particular item.

Checklist of United States Public Documents 1789-1909. Washington, D.C.: Government Printing Office, 1971; reprinted

This is microfilmed reproductions of the U.S. Superintendent of Documents Library shelflist, with supplements.

Catalog of the Public Documents of Congress, 1893-1940.

(Washington, D.C.: Government Printing Office, published irregularly between 1896 and 1945).

Decennial Cumulative Index 1941-1950. 2 vols. (Washington, D.C.: Government Printing Office, 1953). This has been supplemented by an index series published yearly, *Numerical Lists and Schedules of Volumes of the Reports and Documents* for each session of Congress.

OTHER BASIC CONGRESSIONAL DOCUMENTS. *Congress Biographical Directory, 1774-1971.* Washington, D.C.: Government Printing Office, 1972.

Contains names and limited biographies of all members of Congress for the period covered.

Congressional Digest. Washington, D.C.: Congressional Digest Corp., 1921—.

This privately printed monthly publication explores both sides of current controversial topics. After an opening statement of the question under discussion, pro and con arguments drawn from the opinions of experts in that particular field are advanced.

Congressional Directory. Washington, D.C.: Government Printing Office, 1809—.

This directory, which appears with every session of Congress, contains short biographical sketches on all members of the Congress, each of whom is given a limited number of free copies to distribute to his constituents. It also lists the membership of each congressional committee and outlines the committee assignments given each member. One may locate herein the name of his member of Congress, a brief sketch of his or her life, and the boundaries of the district. Information is furnished concerning each member's vote totals in the last several elections.

The major executives of every government agency also are listed, as are members of the diplomatic corps and members of the press who have accredited seating in the congressional press galleries. A pocket edition of this directory contains a photograph of each member of Congress but omits other information.

Congressional Staff Directory. Charles B. Brownson, ed. Mount Vernon, Va.: Congressional Staff Directory, 1959—.

The staffs of individual members of Congress as well as congressional committee staffs have for some time been considered important actors in the political system. Frequently, they are difficult to identify, let alone locate. This source identifies who works for whom and provides basic biographical data on each person.

Guide to the Congress of the United States: Origins, History, and Procedure. 2nd ed. Washington, D.C.: Congressional Quarterly, 1976.

(Annotated in Chapter 3g.)

United States Code and United States Statutes at Large. Washington, D.C.: Government Printing Office, 1875—.

The *United States Code* is published every six years, with an annual supplement. This is the source to consult for a paper on any legislation that has been passed by Congress. It is the source of up-to-date public laws covering every topic. Another source for public laws is *United States Statutes at Large,* a set that breaks down the public laws into two parts: First, all public laws that were passed during a particular year; second, all private bills passed in that year. Laws in both books are classified under 50 titles, such as public lands, education, defense, Congress, and banks.

There are also commercially published editions of the *Code* known as *United States Code Annotated* (St. Paul, Minn.: West, 1927—) and *United States Code Service* (Rochester, N.Y.: The Lawyers Co-Operation Publishing Co. and Bancroft-Whitney Co., 1937—). These annotated editions include notes on judicial interpretations of the law as well as the law itself. If available, they are more useful than the *United States Code.*

If interest lies in state rather than federal laws, the proper source would be individual state codes.

4e Governments, State/Local Documents

American State Governors 1776-1976. 2 vols. Joseph E. Kallenbach and Jessamine S. Kallenbach. Dobbs Ferry, N.Y.: Oceana Publications, 1981.

(Annotated in Chapter 3h.)

American Governors and Gubernatorial Elections, 1775-1978. Roy R. Glashan. Westport, Ct.: Meckler Books, 1979.

(Annotated in Chapter 3h.)

Book of the States. Lexington, Ky.: Council of State Governments, 1970-71—.

Until this edition, it was published under the same title in Chicago: Council of State Governments, 1935—. This biennial work is a rich source of authoritative information on the actual structure, working methods, functioning, and financing of state governments. The legislative, executive, and judicial branches are outlined in depth according to their intergovernmental relations and the major areas of public service performed by each. A directory supplement is published in odd-numbered years.

Important statistics are also contained in these volumes: salaries and compensations of state legislators, divorce laws, voting laws and regulations, state departments, welfare budgets and payments, and educational salaries and budgets.

Constitutions of the United States, National and State Index. Legislative Drafting Service Research Fund, Columbia University. Dobbs Ferry, N.Y.: Oceana, 1962—.

Formerly titled, *Index Digest of State Constitutions,* this digest allows one to compare how each state deals with a particular problem, such as impeachment. It segments each of the 50 state constitutions.

County and City Data Book. Bureau of Census. Washington, D.C.: Government Printing Office, 1952—.

This study has been published every five years since 1965; earlier editions covered staggered time periods from 1949 to 1953. It is basically a supplement to the *Statistical Abstract of the United States,* combining two separate earlier publications, *Cities Supplement* (1944) and *County Data Book* (1947). It covers over 190 items for each county, city and standard metropolitan statistical area in the central states. Items for counties include population, dwelling units, retail trade, wholesale trade, selected service trades, manufacturers, vital statistics, and agricultural units. For city units, government, finances, school systems, hospitals, and climate are added. It also contains similar information classified according to such geographic regions and divisions as states and standard metropolitan statistical areas. Descriptive text and source notes are included.

Directory of Federal Statistics for Local Areas: A Guide to Sources. Urban Update 1977-1978. John D. McCall, ed. Washington, D.C.: Department of Commerce, Bureau of Census, 1980.

One of the most useful federally produced aids in tracking data significant at the state and local levels, this publication is source book to federal sources. If a local political or governmental problem is the topic for research, this directory gives quick access to the most helpful background documents.

How to Get Things Changed: A Handbook for Tackling Community Problems. Bert Strauss and Mary E. Stowe. Garden City, N.Y.: Doubleday, 1974.

The authors base their experience on a federally sponsored community-change project in Virginia. The special values of the book are the concrete suggestions for accomplishing the nitty-gritty aspects of community change, i.e., the idea of using a facilitator rather than a chairperson for a meeting, strategies of organization, etc. The book can be useful also for an academic research paper as a framework or criterion for examining other change efforts.

Index to Current Urban Documents. Westport, Conn.: Greenwood Periodicals, 1972—.

(Annotated in Chapter 2f.)

Legislative Research Checklist. Lexington, Ky.: Council of State Governments, 1947–58; 1959–78; 1980—.

Until 1970 the list was published in Chicago. If writing on an area of domestic public policy, the chances are that some state legislative agency has published a report on the particular topic. This publication helps find it.

Metroplitan Area Annual. Albany, N.Y.: State University at Albany, Graduate School of Public Affairs, 1966—.

Published annually, this work contains the latest developments in municipal government, various city statistics, directories of municipal officials, directories of state agencies functioning at the local level, and facts on metropolitan area planning commissions. The articles summarize developments in a given year.

Monthly Checklist of State Publications. Washington, D.C.: Government Printing Office, 1910—.

A list of approximately 1,500 state publications a month. The documents are arranged by state and carry an annual index.

Municipal Yearbook. Chicago: International City Management Association, 1934—.

This annual reference work is the best source in its field. It is an authoritative resume of activities and statistical data of American cities, with emphasis on individual city programs. Attention is devoted to developments in urban counties and metropolitan areas. It contains thorough bibliographies and comprehensive directories of officials.

The National Directory of State Agencies. Matthew J. Vellucci, Nancy D. Wright, and Gene P. Allen. Washington, D.C.: Information Resources, 1974.

A national listing of state agencies according to sixty-six categories. It also includes associations of state officials. For example, it lists each state agency and official dealing with government support of the arts.

The New York Times Guide to Federal Aid for Cities and Towns. Howard S. Rowland. New York: Quadrangle, 1971.

Tells all one ever wanted to know about grants-in-aid. Starting with a description of the impact of federal grants on one city, Peekskill, New York, the study then describes how to write an aid proposal and provides an in-depth look at the vast range of federal programs. The programs themselves are arranged in topical sections, with an introductory explanation of federal grants. The source is most likely intended for cities seeking grants.

Sage Urban Studies Abstracts. Beverly Hills, Calif.: Sage Publications, 1973—.
  (Annotated in Chapter 2b.)

Selected Bibliography on State Government 1973-1978. Lexington, Ky.:
Council of State Governments, 1979.
  Using author and key-word indexes, the work is oriented toward practical
problems and official reports rather than academic treatment. A selected
bibliography of state government was also published for the years 1959–1972.

State Government Reference Publications: An Annotated Bibliography, 2nd
ed. David W. Parish. Littleton, Colo.: Libraries Unlimited, Inc., 1981.
  (Annotated in Chapter 2d.)

4f ACADEMIC JOURNALS

There are at least three ways that academic journals may be useful in political science research: (1) students may read specific articles in a topic area. The
bridges to these articles are the indexes and the digests and abstracts described
in Chapter 2; (2) students may browse for ideas. By looking through the relevant journals they can locate current research and ideas that might never reach
book form, or if they do, it may be years before they are published; (3) journals
are an avenue to the *professional* aspects of political science. As in the case of
any other profession, political science has its own language and way of thinking. This professional point of view is apt to be very important to your instructor, and these journals are a good introduction to this viewpoint. There are
literally hundreds of possible journals in which students can browse. The most
useful to students, from among those journals considered most familiar and of
highest quality by professional political scientists,[1] are the following, plus a
few periodicals which are relatively new but which promise to fill existing
gaps in the literature.

General Political Science Journals

These scholarly journals tend to emphasize frontier research. To the lay-
person, they may seem remote from the everyday political world, yet they can
be a key source for information and analysis. The following two journals are
regarded as the most prestigious.

American Political Science Review. The American Political Science Association.
1906—. Quarterly.
  The official scholarly journal of the American Political Science Association,
it is considered among the most highly regarded political science journals in

  1. Michael W. Giles and Gerald C. Wright, "Political Scientists' Evaluations of
Sixty-three Journals," *P.S.* 8 (Summer 1975): 255-256.

the field. In recent years it has contained highly methodological articles as well as more process oriented contributions. Sample articles include: "Elite Integration in the United States and Australia," and "Toward a Diachronic Analysis of Congress."

World Politics. Center for International Studies, Princeton University. 1948—. Quarterly.

Regarded as one of the finest political science journals, this quarterly focuses upon international relations and is less concerned with methodological issues than, for example, the *American Political Science Review*. Examples of recent articles include: "The Strategic Triangle: An Elementary Game-Theory Analysis," and "The Soviet Leadership Problem."

Regional Journals

Regional political science associations publish other academically oriented high quality journals. At one time these journals emphasized articles on the politics of their particular region. This is decidedly less so today, but occasionally an issue will focus on regional politics. These journals are as follows:

The Journal of Politics. Southern Political Science Association. 1939—. Quarterly.

The Western Political Quarterly. Western Political Science Association. 1948—. Quarterly.

American Journal of Political Science (formerly *Midwest Journal of Political Science*). Midwest Political Science Association. 1957—. Quarterly.

Polity. Northeastern Political Science Association. 1968—. Quarterly.

Social Science Quarterly. Southwestern Social Science Association cooperatively with the Southwestern Political Science Association. 1920—. Quarterly.

Other General Political Science Journals

Political Science Quarterly. The Academy of Political Science. 1886—. Quarterly.

The major outlet for political science manuscripts in the early days of the discipline in the United States. Today it places more emphasis on historical and normative articles than other more quantitatively oriented journals. Samples of articles include: "Soviet Responses to MX," and "Congress, Courts and Agencies: Equal Employment and Limits of Policy Implementation."

The Annals of the American Academy of Political and Social Science. Sage, 1891—. Bimonthly.

Each issue is devoted to a single topic with its own guest editor. Topics have included: "Gun Control," "The Internationalization of the American Economy," and "International Terrorism."

British Journal of Political Science. Cambridge University Press. 1971—. Quarterly.

Although based in Britain, this journal is designed for a worldwide professional readership. Current emphasis is on articles in political behavior, comparative politics and public policy. Sample articles include: "The Supreme Soviet and Budgetary Politics in the USSR," and "A Probabilistic Approach to the Causes of Coups d' Etat."

International Political Science Review (Revue Internationale de science politique). Sage. 1980—. Quarterly.

The official journal of the International Political Science Association contains articles, original essays, roundtables, colloquia and congresses. Past issues have been devoted to such topics as: "Civil-Military Relations," "Politics and Geography," and "The Biology of Politics."

Journals in Subfields or Closely Related Fields to Political Science

Subject specialist journals are available in a number of political science subfields. Some are interdisciplinary, and contributors may come from a variety of academic fields or may be practitioners.

Foreign Affairs: An American Quarterly Review. Council on Foreign Relations, Inc. 1922—. Quarterly.

The organ of an influential policy-formation group features articles by noted foreign policy practitioners and scholars. Examples of articles of contemporary importance include: "Nuclear Weapons in the 1980s," and "The Mutual Hostage Relationship of the Superpowers."

International Affairs. Royal Institute of International Affairs. 1922—. Quarterly.

A British view of foreign affairs may be found in such articles as "Peace Programme for the 1980s," and "Israeli Aggression Against Lebanon."

Journal of International Affairs. Columbia University, School of International Affairs. 1947—. Semi-annually.

This periodical contains the following type of articles: "United Nations Conference Politics and the New International Order in the Field of Science and Technology," and "External Financing of Development—Challenges and Concerns."

International Organization. World Peace Foundation, MIT Press. 1947—. Quarterly.

Concerned principally with international organizations such as the United Nations, the European Economic Community, and the North Atlantic Treaty Organization, this journal also contains articles on political economy, foreign policy, and comparative politics. Sample articles include: "Weapons Standardization in NATO: Collaborative Security or Economic Competition?" and "Canada's Role in the International Uranium Cartel."

Journal of Conflict Resolution (Formerly: Conflict Resolution). Sage. 1957—. Quarterly.

The major focus of this respected journal is upon conflict within, between, and among nation-states. Most articles display methodological sophistication such as: "Income Inequality and Domestic Violence," and "Spatial Models and Centrality: Meeting Between Arab Leaders."

Comparative Politics. The City University of New York. 1968—. Quarterly.

Among the highly regarded subfield journals this publication contains such articles as "Military Regime Performance: An Appraisal of the Ghana Experience, 1972–1978" and "Theoretical Implications of a Mexican Case Study."

Comparative Political Studies. Sage. 1968—. Quarterly.

Contains the following type of articles: "On Measuring Party System Change: A Methodological Critique and a Suggestion," and "Mass Preferences and Elite Decisions in West Germany."

American Behavioral Scientist. Sage. 1957—. Bimonthly.

An interdisciplinary journal with many articles by political scientists. Sample articles include: "The Politics of Environmental Policy," and "Varieties of Political Conservatism."

Public Opinion Quarterly. Columbia University. 1937—. Quarterly.

Illuminates problems of communication and public opinion. Contains such relevant articles as "Presidents, Prosperity, and Public Opinion," and "Survey Research and Southern Politics: The Implications of Data Management."

Political Behavior. Agathon Press, Inc. 1979—. Quarterly.

Provides a central source of research and theory in the subfields of political sociology and political psychology. Contains such articles as "The Mass Media and Changes in Adolescents' Political Knowledge During an Election Cycle," and "A Logistic Diffusion Model of Political Mobilization."

Biopolitics and the Life Sciences. Association for Politics and the Life Sciences, Northern Illinois University. 1982—. Semi-annually.

A journal devoted to developments in biosocial science. Explores such topics as the influence of biological factors such as drugs, sex, and age on political behavior, and the relationship of biopolitics to the other approaches in political science.

The Review of Politics. University of Notre Dame. 1939—. Quarterly.

Viewing political science from a philosophical and historical perspective this journal features articles such as "The Three Families of Thomas Hobbes," and "Modern Conservatism: The Problem of Definition."

Political Theory: An International Journal of Political Philosophy. Sage. 1973—. Quarterly.

A normative theory journal includes such articles as "The Character and Composition of Aristotle's Politics," and "H.L.A. Hart's Minimum Content Theory of Natural Law."

Politics and Society. Geron-X Inc., 1970—. Quarterly.

Self-described as a radical journal of social science, published articles have included: "Policy Fragmentation and Capitalist Reform: The Defeat of National Land-Use Policy," and "The Workers' Movement and the Bolivian Revolution."

American Politics Quarterly. Sage. 1973—. Quarterly.

Limited to American politics a few sample articles from this journal are: "Executive-Legislative Power Relationships," and "Election Night Projections and West Coast Turnout."

Legislative Studies Quarterly. Comparative Legislative Research Center, The University of Iowa. 1976—. Quarterly.

An international journal with a cross-cultural perspective on representative assemblies publishes articles with titles such as, "Candidate Visibility in France and the United States," and "Factors Influencing the Adoption of New Methods of Legislative Oversight in the U.S. States."

Congress & the Presidency (formerly *Congressional Studies*). American University Center for Congressional and Presidential Studies and the U.S. Capitol Historical Society. 1972— Semiannually.

An interdisciplinary journal of political science and history that presents articles focusing upon the presidency, Congress, interinstitutional conflicts and interactions, and national policy issues. Examples of recent articles include: "Moving Beyond the Oval Office: Problems in Studying the Presidency," and "The Party Going Strong: Congress and Elections in the Mid-19th Century."

Presidential Studies Quarterly. Center for the Study of the Presidency. 1972—. Quarterly.

This journal is devoted to the study of the U.S. presidency. Each issue has a theme such as "Perceptions of the Presidency, Leadership and Statesmanship," and "Separation of Powers and the Power to Govern." Along with numerous articles in each issue, book reviews and editorial essays also appear.

Judicature. American Judicature Society. 1917—. Monthly, except bimonthly in June-July and December-January.

Contains articles, letters, book reviews, and news on all aspects of judicial administration and reform. Sample articles include: "The Central Panel System: Enhancing Administrative Justice;" "Toward Understanding Jury Instructions;" and "Who sets the Pace of Litigation in Urban Trial Courts."

Law and Society Review. Law and Society Association. 1967—. Quarterly.

An interdisciplinary journal brings together lawyers, social scientists, and humanists to focus on law as a social institution. Examples of widely related articles include "Equity and Discretion in a Modern Islamic Legal System," and "Social Status and Sentences of Female Offenders."

Law & Policy Quarterly. Sage. 1979—. Quarterly.

A multidisciplinary journal featuring articles by legal and social science scholars. Sample articles include: "The Evolution of Law and Wife Abuse;" "The Role Concept in Judicial Research;" and "The Federal Rules of Civil Procedure: A Policy Evaluation."

Public Administration Review. American Society for Public Administration. 1940—Bimonthly.

A forum for practitioners and academics, this journal contains such articles as: "Combating Inflation through Wage Negotiations: A Strategy for Public Administration" and "The Cost of Free Service: Organizational Impediments to Access to Public Services."

Administrative Science Quarterly. Cornell University. 1956—. Quarterly.

An interdisciplinary journal devoted to understanding both private and public organizations through the application of social science techniques. Sample articles include: "Power in University Budgeting: A Replication and Extension," and "The Impact of Government Size and Number of Administrative Units on the Quality of Public Service."

Public Choice. Martinus Nijhoff Publishers. 1966—. Quarterly.

Employing economic assumptions and analytical tools, this journal joins political scientists and economists together to feature such articles as "Political Power and the Market for Governors" and "An Empirical Assessment of the Factor-Supplier Pressure Group Hypothesis."

Policy Studies Journal. Policy Studies Organization. 1972—. Quarterly.

Contains symposia on a wide range of public policy matters including such topics as crime, race, sex, transportation, agriculture and national defense. Also publishes issues containing general interest and literature review articles.

Policy Studies Review. Policy Studies Organization. 1981—. Quarterly.

A sister publication of *Policy Studies Journal, PSR* possesses an inter-disciplinary focus containing symposia, refereed articles and book reviews emphasizing implementation and evaluation research.

Public Interest. National Affairs. 1965—. Quarterly.

As the title implies, this journal contains a wide range of articles including, for example, "When Science Progresses and Bureaucracies Lag—the Case of Cancer Research," and "The Global 2000 Controversy."

Urban Affairs Quarterly. Sage. 1965—. Quarterly.

A forum for the interchange of ideas between those engaged in applied and basic urban research. Sample articles include: "Community Power and Policy Outputs: The Routines of Local Politics," and "Characteristics of Support for Local Growth Control."

Publius-The Journal of Federalism. Center for the Study of Federalism, Temple University. 1971—. Quarterly.

Possesses a broad interdisciplinary view of nonsovereign political entities. "Is Federalism Compatible with Prefectorial Administration?" and "Reci-procity, Consumerism and Collective Action" are illustrative of articles con-tained in this journal.

Political Methodology. Geron-X, Inc. 1974—. Quarterly.

This journal focuses on how political inquiry is conducted and innovation employed in the various tools. Sample articles are "Participant Observation in Political Research," and "A Statistical Study of the Cube Law in Five Electoral Systems."

Journals in Other Disciplines Related to Political Science

The following journals all include some politically relevant articles from the perspective of another discipline. Sociology is the other social science discipline most closely related to contemporary political science. Almost all behavior we identify as "political" can be at least partially explained in terms of some sociological concept such as class, race, or bureaucratization. Then, too, political science methods are closely associated with prior developments in sociology and psychology. Note the examples in the following journals. Of course, the roots of political science as a discipline can be found in history and the relevance of the humanities is undeniable.

American Journal of Sociology. The University of Chicago. 1895—. Bimonthly.

Sample articles of interest to political science students are "Competing Models of Political Mobilization: The Role of Ethnic Ties" and "Perspectives on the Legal Order: The Capacity for Social Control."

Social Forces: An International Journal of Social Research. The University of North Carolina Press. 1922—. Quarterly.

Sample articles are "A Marxist Consideration of Durkheim" and "Youth, Voluntary Associations and Political Socialization."

American Sociological Review. American Sociological Association. 1936—. Bimonthly.

Sample articles are "Social Control Theory and Delinquency" and "Racial Tolerance as a Function of Group Position."

Social Science History. Sage. 1976—. Quarterly.

Features relevant theories and methods of the social sciences in an explicit attempt to improve the quality of historical explanation. Contains articles of interest to students of politics in such essays as "Voter Turnout, Critical Elections, and the New Deal Realignment" and "Size and Duration of Empire: Growth and Decline Curves, 600 B.C. to 600 A.D."

Daedalus. American Academy of Arts and Science. 1958—. Quarterly.

The focus is on issues of an interdisciplinary nature with particular emphasis on the humanities. Issues are usually devoted to a particular topic such as "Black Africa: A Generation After Independence," "The End of Consensus" or "U.S. Defense Policy in the 1980s."

5

Footnotes and Bibliography

Few aspects of writing cause as much confusion, bewilderment, and frustration as the proper use of footnotes. They are an essential part of scholarly writing, but until the fundamentals of their use are mastered the footnote requirement can be a constant source of frustration. As a writing device, footnotes are useful because they allow important information to be communicated without overburdening the text. More specifically, they allow a writer to reflect both credit and blame where they are due by showing the source of facts and ideas, thereby permitting the reader to utilize cited sources. In addition, they act as a helpful context for presented information, indicating sources. Finally, footnotes permit a writer to discuss interesting sidelights of the material without breaking the flow of writing.

Two questions invariably arise whenever footnotes are required:
1. What should be footnoted?
2. What form is correct, particularly if unusual or specialized material is being used, such as mimeographed campaign literature?

WHAT TO FOOTNOTE

While most style manuals or term paper handbooks deal with footnote form, they seldom touch upon the more difficult and confusing question of what kind of source should be footnoted and when. It is tempting to "over-document" a paper, to hang footnotes on it as though on a Christmas tree. This approach can be hazardous, for besides wasting time, the reader is overburdened with needless side trips to the bottom of the page, increasing the likelihood of technical errors, and so detracting from the substance of a paper. Unnecessary footnotes, far from being a safeguard, can become a real problem.

Equally hazardous is the practice of "under-documentation," giving rise to the threat of material distortion, i.e., important points may be omitted to avoid documentation, or the source of information and ideas may be left to the reader's imagination, implying that the work of others is somehow one's own. Between these two unfortunate extremes three styles of scholarship are defined: the *original scholar*, the *scholarly summarizer*, and the *essayist and journalist*. The style that most closely approximates the assigned type of paper should be followed. The *original scholar* form is appropriate for doctoral dissertations, master's theses, honors papers, or term papers that fulfill the major portion of the requirements for a course. This style should also be used for papers consisting mainly of scholarly research from primary sources.

The *scholarly summarizer* style is appropriate for more frequently assigned term papers that fulfill a minor portion of the requirements for a course. This type of paper usually consists of a summary, interpretation, and synthesis of secondary sources.

The *essayist and journalist* style is also appropriate for many types of term papers, but in such cases the emphasis is upon the writer's own experience or interpretation. Strictly speaking, there are few ideas that are completely new; however, if the emphasis is to be on an original and creative reaction to these ideas, and not on the ideas themselves or their origin, the essayist style is appropriate. This style may also be used if the paper is primarily a personal account or a narrative of events witnessed or situations in which the writer participated.

Table 5–1 summarizes the use of footnotes for each of the styles of scholarship.

Quotations

Little question exists about the footnoting of direct quotations. The *original scholar* and the *scholarly summarizer* almost always footnote direct quotations.

TABLE 5-1: THREE TYPES OF SCHOLARSHIP AND APPROPRIATE FOOTNOTE USE

Type of Information	Original Scholar	Scholarly Summarizer	Essayist and Journalist
Quotations	All except those quotations of common knowledge, in which case they would still be footnoted if they varied from one edition to another.	Same as original scholar.	Only if the quotation is controversial or highly significant to the text, in which case the reference would be incorporated into the body of the material.
Facts	All but those that are part of common knowledge.	All controversial facts, a representative amount of significant facts to indicate the nature of sources, and only obscure facts that are central to the meaning of the paper.	Only controversial facts central to the meaning of the paper.

The exceptions for even the most scholarly styles are quotations from such items of public domain as the Bible and the United States Constitution. In such cases it is permissible to incorporate a general reference into the text of the material.

Example. There seemed little question that the proposal violated the "equal protection clause," the Fourteenth Amendment to the Constitution. Another example would include: The dogmatic insistence of the neighborhood leader's position reminded one of Henry Clay's, "Sir, I would rather be right than President."

The *essayist and journalist* makes even greater use of the device of incorporating general references into the body of the text.

Example. The writer as a witness or observer: "Sir," Reynaud replied, "we know that you will carry on. We would also if we saw any hope of victory." Winston S. Churchill, *Their Finest Hour, The Second World War* (Boston: Houghton Mifflin, 1949).

Facts

Original scholars footnote all but the most obvious facts. If in doubt they ask themselves if the average mature reader would automatically be aware of the origin and authenticity of a particular fact. If not, it should be footnoted. In general, the three criteria for footnoting facts are:

1. *Controversiality:* Could honest men or women disagree over the authenticity or significance of this fact?
2. *Significance to the paper:* Does a significant part of the argument rest upon this fact?
3. *Obscurity:* Are the means or sources for establishing the authenticity of this fact beyond the average reader's experience or recall?

In general, if a fact could be questioned in a scholarly paper on the basis of any of these three criteria, it should be footnoted.

The *scholarly summarizer* needs to footnote only a representative sampling of the significant facts. In this way the type of sources used is indicated. Obscure facts need not be footnoted unless they are central to the significance of the paper.

The *essayist and journalist* seldom footnotes facts unless they are both controversial and significant to the basic purpose of the paper.

EXPLANATORY OR DISCURSIVE FOOTNOTES

Not every individual will read a report with the same interest. Some readers will be interested only in the main conclusions and the general thread of ideas, while others will be interested in exploring in depth various aspects of the supporting evidence. Still other readers will want to read the interesting sidelights found in research; some will find these sidelights a definite distraction. How is it possible for one manuscript to please such widely varying tastes?

Footnotes that comment upon and interpret data can be a partial solution to this dilemma. Such footnotes can be used for supplementary information that will be of interest to some readers. How often you use such footnotes depends upon the assumptions you hold about your reader. We suggest the following guidelines for each style of scholarship.

Original Scholar

Assume that some of your readers will wish to explore the origins and implications of most of your work. If there are important aspects of your methodology or the content of your research which you are not including in your text, then consider explanatory or discursive footnotes.

Scholarly Summarizer

Assume that your reader will wish to explore the origin and implications of points central to your main thesis or idea. Try to include these points in the body of your text. Therefore, avoid when possible the use of explanatory or discursive footnotes.

Essayist or Journalist

Assume that your readers want to flow smoothly through your paper. Sidetrack them with an explanatory or discursive footnote only if both of the following two conditions are met:
1. There are significantly different interpretations of one of your *major* points.
2. You believe the explanation in your footnote would be of interest to a significant portion of your readers.

When to Use Explanatory or Discursive Footnotes

These footnotes are most often used in the following situations:
(1) *To comment on the importance of a source. Example.* Footnote 61. "One of the landmark studies in the field of business administration is *Strategy and Structure* by A. D. Chandler, Jr.
(2) *To provide background on research methodology. Example.* Footnote 19. For the various methods of calculating indices of interagreement see: Lee F. Anderson, Meredith W. Watts, Jr., and Allen R. Wilcox, *Legislative Roll-Call Analysis* (Evanston: Northwestern University Press, 1966). See also Duncan MacRae, Jr., *Issues and Parties in Legislative Voting: Methods of Statistical Analysis* (New York: Harper and Row, 1970) for a systematic review of the literature relevant to roll-call analysis.

(3) *To trace the origin of an idea or research methodology. Example.*
Footnote 18. Prominent commentary on political obligations was offered by St. Thomas, Locke, Rousseau, and notably T. H. Green, who may have been the first to use the term. A study of Green's thought and environment is Melvin Richter, *The Politics of Conscience: T. H. Green and His Age* (Cambridge, Mass.: Harvard University Press, 1964), pp. 5–57. Also see John Plamenatz, *Consent, Freedom, and Political Obligation,* 2nd ed. (New York: Oxford University Press, 1968).

(4) *To identify summaries of an idea or research methodology. Example.*
Footnote 5. For an interesting review of legal culture research see Austin Sarat, "Studying American Legal Culture: An Assessment of Survey Evidence," *Law and Society Review* 11 (Winter 1977): 427–88.

(5) *To identify the context of a controversial opinion or source. Example.*
Footnote 37. "I rely for this version of the vice-presidential selection on the excellent and exclusive reporting of Carleton Kent, in the *Chicago Sun-Times,* reporting acknowledged by those who were present to be authentic." Theodore H. White, *The Making of the President 1960* (New York: Antheneum, 1961), p. 201.

(6) *To provide additional information on:*
  (a) *The meaning of words. Example.* Footnote 35. *Vybory* is the Russian word meaning, "alternatives." See Jerome M. Gilisin, "Soviet Elections as a Measure of Dissent: The Missing One Percent," *American Political Science Review* 62 (September 1968): 85.
  (b) *A normative problem—normative queries: library sources. Example.* Footnote 24. P. W. Bridgman is generally regarded as the father of the operational philosophy, and his intellectual indebtedness to Bentley is reflected in P. W. Birdgman, "Error, Quantum Theory, and the Observer," *Life, Language, Law: Essays in Honor of Arthur F. Bentley,* edited by Richard W. Taylor (Yellow Springs, Ohio: Antioch Press, 1957), pp. 125–31.
  (c) *Methodology used in the research. Example.* Footnote 23. The political and social characteristics chosen for the chi-square goodness-of-fit test include: age, sex, education, occupation, political party preference, and religious preference.

BIBLIOGRAPHIC VARIATIONS AMONG THREE STYLES

All three styles of scholarship use bibliographies, but a slight variation is present between the scholarly styles and that of the essayist and journalist. Both the *original scholar* and the *scholarly summarizer* place their bibliographic entries in categories of written form. The most common are books, periodicals, newspapers (sometimes combined with periodicals), newspapers (sometimes combined with periodicals), government documents, dissertations, unpublished manuscripts, interviews, and letters. The *essayist and journalist* usually does not have enough citations to justify separate categories and simply lists all sources alphabetically, by the last name of the author. A bibliography should include all works cited in footnotes plus any other works that were used. Works that were examined but proved not particularly relevant should not be cited.

FORMS FOR FOOTNOTES AND BIBLIOGRAPHIES

Footnote and bibliography forms are arbitrary. There is no inherent reason to use one form rather than another, except for the sake of clear communication and consistency. The works used should be cited in the same form as that used in indexes, bibliographies, or library card catalogs. In this way, a reader will be able to locate cited sources.

What follows are examples of the most frequent types of footnotes and bibliographic entries used in a political science paper. Most of the forms are based upon: *A Chicago Manual of Style,* 13th ed., rev. (Chicago: University of Chicago Press, 1983); Kate L. Turabian, *A Manual for Writers of Term Theses and Dissertations,* 4th ed. (Chicago: University of Chicago Press, 1973); and *A Uniform System of Citation,* 13th ed. (Cambridge: Harvard Law Review Association, 1981). The last source was employed only for materials subsumed under the legal citation section on page 131. Although the forms presented are probably consistent with what most instructors require from their students, there is an alternative form of citation gaining prominence within political science circles. That scientific reference format will be dealt with after the examples for the more conventional form of footnote and bibliographical citation.

FOOTNOTES, GENERAL RULES

Books should include:
1. Author's full name (as it appears on the title page of the book)
2. Complete title
3. Editor, compiler, or translator (if any)
4. Name of series, volume or series number (if any)
5. Number of volumes
6. City, publisher, and date of publication
7. Volume number and page number

Articles should include:
1. Author
2. Title of article
3. Periodical
4. Volume of periodical
5. Date of periodical and page numbers of article

Unpublished material should include:
1. Author
2. Title (if any)
3. Type of material
4. Where it may be found
5. Date
6. Page number (if any)

BIBLIOGRAPHY, GENERAL RULES

Footnote style can be changed into bibliographic style by transposing the author's first and last names, removing parentheses from facts of publication, omitting page references, and repunctuating with periods instead of commas.

Books should include:
1. Name of author(s), editors, or responsible institutions
2. Full title, including subtitle if one exists
3. Series (if any)
4. Volume number
5. Edition, if not the original, location and name of publisher
6. Publisher's name (sometimes omitted)
7. Date of publication

Articles should include:
1. Name of author
2. Title of article
3. Name of periodical
4. Volume and number (or date, or both)
5. Pages

BOOKS

Book With One Author
Footnote: 1. Patrick Dunleavy, *Urban Political Analysis: The Politics of Collective Consumption* (London: The Macmillan Press Ltd., 1980), p. 41.
Bibliography: Dunleavy, Patrick. *Urban Political Analysis: The Politics of Collective Consumption*. London: The Macmillan Press Ltd., 1980.

Book With Two Authors
Footnote: 2. Gabriel A. Almond and Sidney Verba, *The Civic Culture: Political Attitudes and Democracy in Five Nations* (Princeton, N.J.: Princeton University Press, 1963), p. 78.

Bibliography: Almond, Gabriel A. and Verba, Sidney. *The Civic Culture: Political Attitudes and Democracy in Five Nations.* Princeton, N.J.: Princeton University Press, 1963.

Book With Three Authors
Footnote: 3 John Henry Merryman, David S. Clark, and Lawrence M. Friedman, *Law and Social Change in Mediterranean Europe and Latin America: A Handbook of Legal and Social Indicators for Comparative Study* (Dobbs Ferry, N.Y.: Oceana Publications, Inc., 1980), p. 17.
Bibliography: Merryman, John Henry; Clark, David S.; and Friedman, Lawrence M. *Law and Social Change in Mediterranean Europe and Latin America: A Handbook of Legal and Social Indicators for Comparative Study.* Dobbs Ferry, N.Y.: Oceana Publications, Inc., 1980.

Book With More Than Three Authors
Footnote: 4. John C. Wahlke, et al., *The Legislative System: Explorations in Legislative Behavior* (New York: John Wiley and Sons, Inc., 1962), p. 111.
Bibliography: Wahlke, John C.; Eulau, Heinz; Buchanan, William; and Ferguson, Leroy C. *The Legislative System: Explorations in Legislative Behavior.* New York: John Wiley and Sons, Inc., 1962.

Edition of Book other than First
Footnote: 5. Lawrence C. Dodd and Bruce I. Oppenheimer, *Congress Reconsidered,* 2d ed. (Washington, D.C.: Congressional Quarterly Press, 1981), p. 119.
Bibliography: Dodd, Lawrence C. and Oppenheimer, Bruce I. *Congress Reconsidered.* 2d ed. Washington, D.C.: Congressional Quarterly Press, 1981.

Book in a Series
Footnote: 6. Richard Rose, *Politics in England,* The Little, Brown Series in Comparative Politics (Boston: Little, Brown and Co., 1964), p. 83.
Bibliography: Rose, Richard. *Politics in England.* The Little, Brown Series in Comparative Politics. Boston: Little, Brown and Co., 1964.

Book by Editor or Transalator:
Editors
Footnote: 7. E. Owen Smith, ed., *Trade Unions in the Developed Economies* (London: Croom Helm Ltd., 1981), p. 89.
Bibliography: Smith, E. Owen, ed. *Trade Unions in the Developed Economies.* London: Croom Helm Ltd., 1981.

Book with a Translator
Footnote: 8.   Ernest Mandel, *Introduction to Marxism,* Trans. Louisa Sadler (London: Ink Links, Ltd., 1979), p. 59.
Bibliography: Mandel, Ernest. *Introduction to Marxism.* Translated by Louisa Sadler. London: Ink Links, Ltd., 1979.
Comment: When the author's and translator's names both appear on the title page, the translator's name should appear after the title. However, if the author's name is not on the title page, the translator's name should appear first, followed by the word trans.

Book, Multivolume
Footnote: 9.   Carl Sandburg, *Abraham Lincoln: The War Years,* 4 vols. (New York: Harcourt, Brace and Co., 1939), 1: 113.
Bibliography: Sandburg, Carl. *Abraham Lincoln: The War Years.* Vol. 1. New York: Harcourt, Brace and Co., 1939.

Citation in One Book from Another Book
Footnote: 10.   E.E. Schattshneider, *Party Government,* pp. 131–32. As quoted ·in Frank J. Sorauf, *Party Politics in America,* 4th ed. (Boston: Little, Brown and Co., 1980), p. 325.
Bibliography: Sorauf, Frank J. *Party Politics in America.* 4th ed. Boston: Little, Brown and Co., 1980.

Book Review
Footnote: 11.   William R. Garner, Review of *Mexico's Political Leaders: Their Education and Recruitment* by Roderic A. Camp, *The Journal of Politics* 43 (August, 1981): 952.
Bibliography: Garner, William R. Review of *Mexico's Political Leaders: Their Education and Recruitment* by Roderic A. Camp. *The Journal of Politics* 43 (August, 1981): 952.
Comment: The first name cited is that of the reviewer of the book. The second name cited is the author of the book.

Classical Works
Footnote: 12.   Julius Caesar, *The Conquest of Gaul* 1., 2–4.
Bibliography: Caesar, Julius. *The Conquest of Gaul* 1.

Modern Edition of Classical Work
Footnote: 13.   Plato, *The Republic,* trans. B. Jowett 5., 452.
Bibliography: Plato. *The Republic.* Translated by B. Jowett.

Book In a Series, One Author, Several Volumes, Each With a Different Title
Footnote: 14.   Arthur M. Schlesinger, *The Age of Roosevelt,* 3 vols., *The Politics of Upheaval* (Boston: Houghton Mifflin, 1960), 3: 56.

Bibliography: Schlesinger, Arthur M. *The Age of Roosevelt.* Vol. 3. *The Politics of Upheaval.* Boston: Houghton Mifflin, 1960.

Paperback Edition of Book First Published in Hard Cover
Footnote: 15. Theodore J. Lowi, *The End of Liberalism: The Second Republic of the United States,* 2d ed. (New York: W. W. Norton and Co., paperback, 1979), p. 277.
Bibliography: Lowi, Theodore J. *The End of Liberalism: The Second Republic of the United States.* 2d ed. Paperback. New York: W. W. Norton and Co., 1979.

Introduction or Foreword to Book by Another Author
Footnote: 16. Chester I. Barnard, Foreword to *Administrative Behavior: A Study of Decision-Making Processes in Administrative Organization,* 3d ed. by Herbert A. Simon (New York: The Free Press, 1976), p. xiii.
Bibliography: Barnard, Chester I. Foreword to *Administrative Behavior: A Study of Decision-Making Processes in Administrative Organization.* 3rd ed. by Herbert A. Simon. New York: The Free Press, 1976.
Comment: The first appearing name is the person writing the foreword or introduction to the book. It is his or her comments which are being footnoted, not those of author of the book.

Book With an Association As Author
Footnote: 17. American Bar Association Special Constitutional Convention Study Committee, *Amendment of the Constitution By the Convention Method Under Article V* (Chicago: American Bar Association, 1974), p. 72.
Bibliography: American Bar Association Special Constitutional Convention Study Committee. *Amendment of the Constitution By the Convention Method Under Article V.* Chicago: American Bar Association, 1974.

Author's Name Not on Title Page, but Known
Footnote: 18. [Alexander Hamilton, James Madison, and John Jay], *The Federalist* (New York: The Modern Library, 1941), p. 53.
Bibliography: [Hamilton, Alexander; Madison, James; and Jay, John.] *The Federalist.* New York: The Modern Library, 1941.

Article, Chapter, or Other Part of a Book
Footnote: 19. Charles E. Lindblom, "The Science of 'Muddling Through,'" *Perspectives on Public Bureaucracy,* 3rd ed., edited by Fred A. Kramer (Cambridge, Mass.: Winthrop Publishers, Inc., 1981), p. 182.

Bibliography: Kramer, Fred A., ed. *Perspectives on Public Bureaucracy,* 3rd ed. Cambridge, Mass.: Winthrop Publishers, Inc. 1981.

Pseudonym, Author's Real Name Known
Footnote: 20. George Tichnor Curtis [Peter Boylston], *The Constitutional History of the United States, From the Declaration of Independence to the Close of Their Civil War* (New York: Harper and Brothers, 1889), p. 25.
Bibliography: Curtis, George Tichnor [Peter Boylston]. *The Constitutional History of the United States, From the Declaration of Independence to Their Civil War.* New York: Harper and Brothers, 1889.
Comment: The pseudonym is placed in brackets.

Book's Author Anonymous
Footnote: 21. *The Holy Quran* (Washington, D.C.: Islamic Center, 1960), p. 59.
Bibliography: *The Holy Quran.* Washington, D.C.: Islamic Center, 1960.
Comment: Avoid use of "Anon." or "Anonymous."

LITERATURE

Novels
Footnote: 22. Robert Ludlum, *The Parsifal Mosaic* (New York: Random House, 1982), chap. 4.
Bibliography: Ludlum, Robert. *The Parsifal Mosaic.* New York: Random House, 1982.
Comment: Because novels often appear in a variety of editions it is best to cite chapter rather than page numbers. However, it is permissible to cite page numbers if the full facts of publication (place, publisher, date) are carefully noted.

Plays and Long Poems
Footnote: 23. Henrik Ibsen, *Hedda Gabler,* act 1, sc. 1, lines 10–18.
Bibliography: Ibsen, Henrik. *Hedda Gabler.*
Comment: For plays and long poems cite as much specific information as possible, *e.g.,* act, part, canto, scene, stanza, line.

Short Poems
Footnote: 24. William Blake, "Mock on, Mock on, Voltaire, Rousseau," stanza 2, line 4.
Bibliography: Blake, William. "Mock on, Mock on, Voltaire, Rousseau."
Comment: Note that for classic works in literature it is not necessary to cite the facts of publication (place, publisher, date). Modern works should, however, include such information.

Bible
Footnote: 25. Ecclesiastes 1: 2–3.
Bibliography: *The Bible.*
Comment: Note that biblical references include chapter and verse, not page numbers.

JOURNAL OR MAGAZINE ARTICLES

Periodical: Author Given
Footnote: 26. M. Stephen Weatherford, "Interpersonal Networks and Political Behavior," *American Journal of Political Science* 26 (February 1982): 131.
Bibliography: Weatherford, M. Stephen. "Interpersonal Networks and Political Behavior." *American Journal of Political Science* 26 (February 1982): 117–143.

Magazine Article, No Author Given
Footnote: 27. "Crown Prince: More Than an Heir," *Time,* 28 June 1982, p. 23.
Bibliography: "Crown Prince: More Than an Heir." *Time,* 28 June 1982, p. 23.

Magazine Article, Author Given
Footnote: 28. Thomas Griffith, "Quality in the Off-Hours," *Time,* September 6, 1982, p. 73.
Bibliography: Griffith, Thomas. "Quality in the Off-Hours." *Time,* September 6, 1982, pp. 73–74.

NEWSPAPERS

Footnote: 29. "Minority Groups Are Reported On Short Side of Senate Votes," *The New York Times,* 21 June 1982, p. 7.
Bibliography: "Minority Groups are Reported On Short Side of Senate Votes." *The New York Times,* 21 June 1982, p. 7.
Comment: When author byline is presented, name author at beginning of citation. For foreign newspapers in which the city is not part of the title place the city name in parentheses, e.g., *Le Monde* (Paris).

ENCYCLOPEDIAS, ALMANACS, AND OTHER REFERENCE WORKS

Signed Articles
Footnote: 30. *International Encyclopedia of the Social Sciences,* 5th ed., s.v. "Political Anthropology: The Field," by Elizabeth Colson.

Bibliography: *International Encyclopedia of the Social Sciences.* 5th ed. s.v.
               "Political Anthropology: The Field," by Elizabeth Colson.

Unsigned Articles
Footnote: 31. *Information Please Almanac 1982,* s.v. "Presidential Elections,
               1789 to 1980."
Bibliography: *Information Please Almanac 1982.* s.v. "Presidential Elections,
               1789 to 1980."
Comment: When citing these type of reference works the place of publica-
               tion, publisher, date, and page numbers are normally omitted.
               However, editions other than the first should be specified. The
               letters s.v. mean *sub verbo,* "under the word."

Material from Manuscript Collections
Footnote: 32. Administration of Justice and Courts, 1916—, Richard Richards
               Papers, Library of University of California, Los Angeles, Calif.,
               p. 3.
Bibliography: Los Angeles, Calif. Library of University of California, Los
               Angeles, Administration of Justice and Courts, 1916—. Richard
               Richards Papers.

Radio and Television Programs
Footnote: 33. NBC, *NBC Nightly News,* 5 December 1979, "Iranian Crisis,"
               Hilary Brown, reporter.
Bibliography: NBC. *NBC Nightly News.* 5 December 1979. "Iranian Crisis."
               Hilary Brown, reporter.

Interview
Footnote: 34. Interview with Senator Alan Dixon, U.S. Senator for the State
               of Illinois, Washington, D.C., January 25, 1982.
Bibliography: Dixon, Alan. U.S. Senator for the State of Illinois. Washington,
               D.C. Interview, 25 January 1982.

Letters
Footnote: 35. Lawrence to Barr, 8 November 1958, Political Papers of Gover-
               nor David Leo Lawrence, Hillman Library, University of Pitts-
               burgh, Pittsburgh, Pa.
Bibliography: Pittsburgh, Pa. Hillman Library, University of Pittsburgh.
               Political Papers of Governor David Leo Lawrence. Lawrence
               to Barr, 8 November 1958.

Mimeographed or Other Nonprinted Reports
Footnote: 36. David R. Derge, "Public Leadership in Indiana," mimeo-
               graphed (Bloomington, Ind., June, 1969), p. 55.

Bibliography: Derge, David R. "Public Leadership in Indiana." Blooming-
ton, Ind., June, 1969.

Pamphlet
Footnote: 37. Mary H. Curzan, ed., *Careers and the Study of Political Science,*
2d ed. (Washington, D.C.: American Political Science Associa-
tion, 1976), p. 19.
Bibliography: Curzan, Mary H., ed. *Careers and the Study of Political Science.*
2d ed. Washington, D.C.: American Political Science Asso-
ciation, 1976.

Proceedings of a Meeting or Conference: Reproduced
Footnote: 38. Annual Report of the American Bar Association Including Proceedings of the Ninety-Ninth Annual Meeting, "Report of the
Standing Committee on Judicial Selection, Tenure and Compensation," (Atlanta, Ga.: August 9–12, 1976), p. 772.
Bibliography: Annual Report of the American Bar Association Including Proceedings of the Ninety-Ninth Annual Meeting, "Report of the
Standing Committee on Judicial Selection, Tenure and Compensation." Atlanta, Ga.: August 9–12, 1976.

Paper Read or Speech Delivered at a Meeting
Footnote: 39. John S. Jackson, III and Barbara Leavitt Brown, "The Rule
Making and Party Reform Functions from the Perspective of
National Convention Delegates: 1974–76–78" (Paper delivered
at the 1979 meeting of the Southern Political Science Associa-
tion, Gatlinburg, Tenn., November 1–3, 1979), p. 12.
Bibliography: Jackson, John S., III and Brown, Barbara Leavitt. "The Rule
Making and Party Reform Functions from the Perspective of
National Convention Delegates: 1974–76–78." Paper delivered
at the 1979 Meetings of the Southern Political Science Asso-
ciation, November 1–3, 1979, at Gatlinburg, Tenn.

Thesis or Dissertation
Footnote: 40. Thomas A. Schwartz, "A Reconceptualization of the First
Amendment: The Burger Court and Freedom of the Press,
1969–1980" (Ph.D. Dissertation, Southern Illinois University,
Carbondale, 1981), p. 131.
Bibliography: Schwartz, Thomas A. "A Reconceptualization of the First
Amendment: The Burger Court and Freedom of the Press,
1969–1980." Ph.D. Dissertation, Southern Illinois University,
Carbondale, 1981.

GOVERNMENT DOCUMENTS

Because the form is totally unlike that of books and magazines, proper government document citation is a difficult problem. The card catalog is a good guide, and the following general rules should help. Include in this order the following:

1. The country or jurisdiction (e.g., U.S., Ill.)
2. The branch of government (legislative, executive, judicial)
3. The subbranch or subbranches of government (e.g., House, Committee on Education and Labor).

Determining the branches or subbranches is not always immediately apparent. However, a careful examination of the document itself, its entry in the card catalog, or in the *Government Organization Manual* should give an idea as to the sequence of organization.

This information is followed by the title (underlined), the name of the series or sequence, and the facts of publication meaning the place of publication, the publisher, and the date of publication. The following examples include some of the most commonly cited government publications.

Congressional Documents

Bills

Footnote: 41. U.S., Congress, House, *Clean Air Act,* H.R. 5252, 97th Cong., 2nd sess., 1982, pp. 1–3.

Bibliography: U.S. Congress. House. *Clean Air Act.* H.R. 5252, 97th Cong., 2nd sess., 1982.

Footnote: 42. U.S., Congress, Senate, *National Nuclear Waste Policy Act,* S.1662, 97th Cong., 2nd sess., 1982, p. 2.

Bibliography: U.S. Congress. Senate. *National Nuclear Waste Policy Act.* S. 1662, 97th Cong., 2nd sess., 1982.

Debates

Footnote: 43. U.S. Congress, Senate, Senator Proxmire Explanation for Voting Against Budget Resolution, 97th Cong., 2d sess., 22 June 1982, *Congressional Record* 128: S 7279.

Bibliography: U.S. Congress. Senate. Senator Proxmire Explanation for Voting Against Budget Resolution. 97th Cong., 2d sess., 22 June 1982. *Congressional Record,* vol. 128, no. 80.

Report

Footnote: 44. U.S. Congress, Senate, *Criminal Code Reform Act of 1981,* S. Rept. 97–307 to accompany S. 1630 97th Cong., 1st sess., 1981.

Bibliography: U.S. Congress. Senate. *Criminal Code Reform Act of 1981.* S. Rept. 97–307 to accompany S. 1630. 97th Cong., 1st sess. 1981.

Hearings

Footnote: 45. U.S., Congress, Senate, Committee on the Judiciary, *Antitrust Procedural Act of 1979, S. 390, Hearings before the subcommittee on Antitrust and Monopoly of the Senate Committee on the Judiciary on S. 390,* 96th Cong., 1st sess., 1979, pp. 55–57.

Bibliography: U.S. Congress. Senate. Committee on the Judiciary. *Antitrust Procedural Act of 1979, S. 390. Hearings before the subcommittee on Antitrust and Monopoly of the Senate Committee on the Judiciary on S. 390.* 96th Cong., 1st sess., 1979.

Executive Documents

From an Executive Department

Footnote: 46. U.S., Department of Commerce, International Trade Administration, *Attracting Foreign Investment to the United States: A Guide for Government* (Washington, D.C.: U.S. Government Printing Office, 1981), p. 41.

Bibliography: U.S. Department of Commerce. International Trade Administration. *Attracting Foreign Investment to the United States: A Guide for Government.* Washington, D.C.: U.S. Government Printing Office, 1981.

Footnote: 47. U.S., Department of State, *Annual Report of the Inspector General of the Department of State and Foreign Service,* Department of Foreign Service Series 305, Department of State Publication 9267 (May 1982), pp. 2–5.

Bibliography: U.S. Department of State. *Annual Report of the Inspector General of the Department of State and Foreign Service.* Department of Foreign Service Series 305, Department of State Publication 9267 (May 1982).

Comment: Many executive department documents carry a publication and/or a publication series number. It is a good idea to include such information in citations. Also, some executive documents contain author names. Although it is permissible to cite author names it is not always practical; libraries often catalog the name of the sponsoring government agency and not author names.

Presidential Papers

Footnote: 48. U.S. President, "Remarks at a Luncheon Meeting with President Alessandro Pertini, June 7, 1982," *Weekly Compilation*

of *Presidential Documents,* vol. 18, no. 23, June 14, 1982, p. 762.
Bibliography: U.S. President. "Remarks at a Luncheon Meeting with President Alessandro Pertini, June 7, 1982." *Weekly Compilation of Presidential Documents.* June 14, 1982.

International Documents

Organizations
Footnote: 49. League of Nations, Economic Intelligence Service, *Balances of Payments 1937* (II.A. 18) (November 1938), p. 191.
Bibliography: League of Nations. Economic Intelligence Service. *Balances of Payments 1937* (II.A. 18) (November 1938).

Footnote: 50. United Nations, Department of International Economic and Social Affairs, *Yearbook of Construction Statistics 1972-1979* (ST/ESA/STAT/SER.U/8), 1982, p. 212.
Bibliography: United Nations. Department of International Economic and Social Affairs. *Yearbook of Construction Statistics 1972-1979* (ST/ESA/STAT/SER.U/8), 1982.

Footnote: 51. United Nations, General Assembly, *Second Committee, Summary Record of the 8th Meeting held on Monday, 6 October 1980,* (A/C.2/35/SR.8), p. 4.
Bibliography: United Nations. General Assembly. *Second Committee, Summary Record of the 8th Meeting held on Monday, 6 October 1980.* (A/C.2/35/SR.8).

Footnote: 52. United Nations, Security Council, *Report of the Security Council Committee Established by Resolution 421 (1977) Concerning the Question of South Africa* (S/13721), 31 December 1979, p. 153.
Bibliography: United Nations. Security Council. *Report of the Security Council Committee Established by Resolution 421 (1977) Concerning the Question of South Africa* (S/13721), 31 December 1979.

Footnote: 53. United Nations, General Assembly, November 20, 1959, *General Assembly Resolution 1386,* A/4353, Annex 16, pp. 19–21.
Bibliography: United Nations. General Assembly. 14th Session, November 20, 1959. *General Assembly Resolution 1386,* A/4353.

Footnote: 54. United Nations, Department of Public Information, *Yearbook of the United Nations 1977,* p. 1051.
Bibliography: United Nations. Department of Public Information. *Yearbook of the United Nations 1977.*

Comment: Turabian suggests that the following elements be presented
              for each international document citation: authorizing body,
              paper topic, document or series number if available, and date.

Treaties
Footnote: 55. U.S., *Statutes at Large,* vol. 59, pt. 2 (1945), "Surrender of
               Japan," 2 September 1945.
Bibliography: U.S. *Statutes at Large,* vol. 59, pt. 2 (1945). "Surrender of
               Japan," 2 September 1945.
Comment: Note that the citation of a treaty found in *Statutes at Large* is
               different for nontreaties, see footnote 63.

Footnote: 56. U.S., Department of State, *United States Treaties and Other
               International Agreements,* vol. 31, pt. 1, "Japan—Extradi-
               tion," TIAS No. 9625, 3 March 1978.
Bibliography: U.S. Department of State. *United States Treaties and Other
               International Agreements,* vol. 31, pt. 1. "Japan-Extradition,"
               TIAS No. 9625, 3 March 1978.

Footnote: 57. United Nations, Treaty Series, *Treaties and International Agree-
               ments Registered or Filed and Recorded with the Secretariat
               of the United Nations,* vol. 948 (1974), No. 13492, "Finland
               and Poland: Agreement Relating to Performance of Rescue
               Operations on the Finnish and Polish Territorial Waters (with
               protocol)," 8 March 1973.
Bibliography: United Nations, Treaty Series. *Treaties and International Agree-
               ments Registered or Filed and Recorded with the Secretariat
               of the United Nations,* vol. 948 (1974), No. 13492, "Finland
               and Poland: Agreement Relating to Performance of Rescue
               Operations on the Finnish and Polish Territorial Waters (with
               protocol)," 8 March 1973.
Comment: Since 1950, U.S. treaties may be found in *United States Treaties
               and Other International Agreements.* The United Nations and
               its predecessor, League of Nations, have treaty series which
               are additional sources for treaties and international agreements.

State and Local Documents

State
Footnote: 58. Illinois, Secretary of State, *Handbook of Illinois Government,*
               June 1981, p. 99.
Bibliography: Illinois. Secretary of State. *Handbook of Illinois Government.*
               June 1981.

Footnote: 59. Illinois, *Constitution,* art. 8, sec. 3.
Bibliography: Illinois. *Constitution.*

Comment: Provide the date of the constitution if the constitution cited
              is not one currently in force, *e.g.,* Illinois, *Constitution* (1848),
              art. 1, sec. 2.

City
Footnote: 60.   Carbondale, Illinois, City Manager, "City of Carbondale, Illi-
              nois Annual Budget FY 1979–80," mimeographed (April 9,
              1979), pp. 23–27.
Bibliography: Carbondale, Illinois. City Manager. "City of Carbondale, Illi-
              nois Annual Budget FY 1979–80." April 9, 1979.
Comment: In general, citations for state and local government documents
              should follow the form for U.S. federal documents. Researchers
              will often encounter insufficient documentation for state and
              local materials. Improvise when necessary because many of
              these materials are not cataloged.

LEGAL CITATIONS

Bibliographic entries for legal citations need not differ from the footnote
format. Bibliography examples are presented for those writers preferring to
distinguish between the two forms.

Court Cases
Footnote: 61.   Dunaway v. New York, 442 U.S. 200 (1978).
Bibliography: Dunaway v. New York. 442 U.S. 200 (1978).
Footnote: 62.   United States v. Grundy, 7 U.S. (3 Cranch) 337 (1806).
Bibliography: United States v. Grundy. 7 U.S. (3 Cranch) 337 (1806).
Comment: The number preceding the letters U.S. refers to the volume,
              while the number following U.S. indicates the first page in the
              volume of *United States Reports* at which the named case
              appears. Early volumes of the *U.S. Reports* included the court
              reporter's name, in our example the name of William Cranch.

Statutes
Footnote: 63.   *Foreign Service Act of 1980,* Publ. L. No. 96–465§ 301, 94
              Stat. 2083 (1980).
Bibliography: *Foreign Service Act of 1980.* Publ. L. No. 96–465§ 301, 94
              Stat. 2083 (1980).
Comment: The first entry, *"Foreign Service Act. . ."* is the title of the
              law; Publ. L. No. 96–465 refers to the official congressional
              public law number assigned this particular piece of legislation.
              The sign (§) means section number. In this case reference is
              to section 301 of the "Foreign Service Act of 1980" titled,
              "General Provisions Relating to Appointments." The number

94 is the volume number of the multivolume *United States Statutes at Large* in which this law is found, and the number 2083 is the page number in that volume where all of the above is located. The date (1980) refers to the time of the legislation.

Code
Footnote: 64. *Comprehensive Employment and Training Act*, 29 U.S.C. (1978) § 834 (Supp. IV 1980).
Bibliography: *Comprehensive Employment and Training Act*. 29 U.S.C. (1978) § 834 (Supp. IV 1980).
Comment: The first entry, "*Comprehensive Employment. . .*" is the name of the law being cited. The number 29 refers to the Title (Labor) in the Code in which this particular law is found. U.S.C. is the standard abbreviation for *United States Code*. The date (1978) refers to the date of passage of the law being cited. The section number (834) pertains to the section of the law being cited, in this case the section dealing with discrimination. The last entry (Supp. IV 1980) refers to the 1980 Supplement volume to the *U.S. Code* in which the material is found.

Law Periodicals
Footnote: 65. Cole, *The Political Impact of Constitutional Courts: A Critique*, 49 NOTRE DAME LAWYER 1046 (1974).
Bibliography: Cole, R. Taylor. *The Political Impact of Constitutional Courts: A Critique*. 49 NOTRE DAME LAWYER, 1045–1050. (1974).
Comment: Note that law journal citations are vastly different from social science journal references.

Constitution
Footnote: 66. U.S. Const. art. I, § 1.
Bibliography: *Need not reference in bibliography.

SECOND OR LATER REFERENCES TO FOOTNOTES

The possibility exists that several references will be made to the same footnote. The general rules on such occasions are as follows:

1. For references to the same work with no intervening footnotes simply use the Latin abbreviation "Ibid.," meaning "in the same place."
2. For second references with no intervening footnote, but with a different page of the same work, state: Ibid., and the page number. Example: Ibid., p. 87.
3. For second references with intervening footnotes, state: the author's last name, but not first name or initials unless another author of the

same name is cited; a shortened title of the work; and the specific page number.

Following are examples of second citations of a representative number of works.

Second References with Intervening Citations

Book
First Citation: 1. Phillip L. Gianos, *Political Behavior: Metaphors and Models of American Politics* (Pacific Palisades, Calif.: Palisades Publishers, 1982), p. 38.
Second Citation: 6. Gianos, *Political Behavior,* p. 219.

Journal Article
First Citation: 3. Edward S. Malecki, "The Capitalist State: Structural Variation and Its Implications for Radical Change," *The Western Political Quarterly* 34 (June 1981): 250.
Second Citation: 9. Malecki, "The Capitalist State," p. 261.

Classical
First Citation: 2. Thucydides, *History of the Peloponnesian War* 4. 14–19.
Second Citation: 10. Thucy. 5. 87–89.

Federal Documents
First Citation: 12. U.S. Congress, Senate, Senator Proxmire Explanation for Voting Against Budget Resolution, 97th Cong., 2d sess., 22 June 1982, *Congressional Record* 128: S 7279.
Second Citation: 15. U.S. Congress, Senate, Proxmire Explanation, S 7280.

Court Case
First Citation: 20. Gannett Co. v. DePasquale, 443 U.S. 368 (1979).
Second Citation: 25. 443 U.S. at 391. *Or* 443 U.S. 368, 391.

SCIENTIFIC REFERENCE FORM

Some political science journals have adopted what is commonly referred to as the scientific reference format. Instead of conventionally numbered footnotes, scientific notations employ in text lines parenthetical references which include the author's last name, the year of publication, and the pagination; *i.e.,* [Possessing experience in complex interactions, lawyers and business people are more likely than others to have an appreciation for bargaining, compromise, and generally the art of the possible (Eulau and Sprague, 1964: 144).]. Today all political science journals published by Sage Publications, Inc.

employ this method, and *The American Political Science Review* and *The Western Political Quarterly* have switched from the conventional format described earlier to the scientific reference style outlined in the remainder of the chapter.

Increasingly, political science instructors are either permitting or encouraging the adoption of the scientific style for student papers. As can be observed from the few examples presented below the scientific format is less difficult to type than the conventional format. Its principal disadvantage is the interruption to the flow of ideas and sentences caused by the intrusion in the body of the text of author names, publication dates, and pagination. The exact format for scientific reference varies somewhat from journal to journal and from one scientific discipline to another. The format recommended below is a hybrid form planned to yield minimum confusion.

Guide to Scientific References

1. All but explanatory footnotes (discursive comments) are placed in the body of the text.
2. Parenthetical references include author, year of publication, and pagination.
3. Repeat earlier citation for second or later references.
4. All sources cited in the text are listed at the end of the paper under the title, REFERENCES.
5. Explanatory or discursive comments are referenced in the conventional reference style with footnote numbers placed in the body of the text and the comments placed together at the end of the manuscript immediately before the REFERENCES. Title the explanatory or discursive comments, NOTES.

Author's name not in body of text
Comment: Author's last name is followed by a comma, the year of publication, colon, and page number if referencing a particular page(s).
Example: . . . conventional wisdom supports the proposition that lawyers exercise considerable influence as the high priests of American politics (Matthews, 1954:30).

More than One Author
Comment: Simply join the two names with the conjunctive "and." If more than two authors employ "et al."
Example: (Schmidhauser and Berg, 1972:191).
Example: (Brady et al., 1973:870).

Multiple References
Comment: Often researchers point to several texts supporting the same or similar statement. In such instances, references are joined by semicolons.
Example: However, in recent years several roll call studies indicate that lawyer-legislators do not vote as a cohesive bloc (Derge, 1959; Schmidhauser and Berg, 1972; Brady et al., 1973).

Author's name in the body of text
Comment: When the author's name is in the body of the text follow the name with the year and pagination.
Example: Scheingold (1974: 13–22) points out that law as an ideology creates. . . .

References to same author and same year
At times scholars will publish several articles or books in the same year and the paper writer may want to cite some or all of the works without confusing which text is being referenced. This problem is eliminated by inserting "a," "b," "c," and so forth in both the *manuscript* and *references* at the end of the paper.
Example: (Schmidhauser, 1973a: 183).
(Schmidhauser, 1973b: 17).
(Schmidhauser, 1973c: 401).

Court Cases Cited in Body of Text
Comment: As with other references, judicial opinions should be referenced in the body of the text. The case name is underlined (italized) followed by the date in parenthesis. For second and later references repeat the case name but delete the date.
Example: . . . the opinion in *Heart of Atlanta Motel* v. *United States* (1964) based the constitutionality of the Civil Rights Act of 1964 upon the Commerce Clause and not the Equal Protection Clause of the Fourteenth Amendment.

References at the End of the Paper
All cited materials are listed together at the end of the paper in alphabetical order by author. In a BIBLIOGRAPHY all relevant sources consulted in researching and writing the paper are included. However, in a REFERENCE only those materials actually cited in the text of the paper are included. Also, this rule applies to books or articles with three or more authors as well as works with a lesser number of authors. The reference form for articles, books, associations as author, and dissertations or theses differ. Note each in the sample references presented below.

Judicial opinions should be listed in alphabetical order with full citation to volume, reporter series, page and date. This list should appear immediately following the REFERENCES at the end of the paper under the separate title, CASES CITED.

Books:
Durkheim, Emile (1958). *Professional Ethics and Civil Morals.* Glencoe: Free Press.
Eulau, Heinz and John D. Sprague (1964). *Lawyers in Politics: A Study of Professional Convergence.* Indianapolis: Bobbs-Merrill.
McLaughlin, Andrew Cunningham (1972a). *The Courts, the Constitution, and Parties: Studies in Constitutional History and Politics.* New York: Da Capo Press.
_____ (1972b). *The Foundations of American Constitutionalism.* Gloucester, Mass.: P. Smith.

Articles:
Dyer, James A., (1976). "Do Lawyers Vote Differently? A Study of Voting on No-Fault Insurance." *Journal of Politics* 38 (May): 452–456.
Green, Justin J., John R. Schmidhauser, Larry L. Berg, and David Brady (1973). "Lawyers in Congress: A New Look at Some Old Assumptions." *Western Political Quarterly* 26 (September): 440–452.

Association:
American Bar Association (1975). *Report of American Bar Association.* Chicago: American Bar Foundation.

Theses or Dissertations:
Wells, Richard Sutton (1963). "The Legal Profession and Political Ideology: The Case of the Carr Law Firm of Manchester, Iowa." Ph.D. dissertation. Iowa City: University of Iowa.

Cases Cited:
Heart of Atlanta Motel v. United States, 379 U.S. 241, 1964.
Wickard, Secretary of Agriculture, et al. v. Filburn, 317 U.S. 111, 1942.

6

Special Skills and Additional Information

WRITING A LETTER TO THE EDITOR

Most newspapers have a letter-to-the-editor column, which they run as they see fit—once a week, several times a week, or daily.

This is one way of corresponding with your representatives in Washington and your state capital. It is also an excellent way of shaking out an issue within the circulation area of the newspaper; chances are, your letter will draw pro and con responses from your fellow readers. And it has been said that, when your letter appears in print, the chances are strong that you are addressing the largest audience you will ever have in your life.

Here are a few tips to help your letter find its way past the editor's desk and into print:

1. If possible, use a typewriter, double space, and type on only one side of the paper.
2. Be clear and as brief as possible. If you ramble on for 500 words, your letter is sure to be cut drastically, and you might even lose the opportunity to get into print.
3. Focus on a single topic for each letter; make sure it is timely, even newsworthy.
4. Hone that first sentence to a good edge; grab the editor's attention quickly.
5. If you are criticizing, take some of the sting from your complaint by adding a word of praise, appreciation, or agreement. End the letter with some constructive suggestions.
6. Be calm. Do not rant or use abusive or violent language. That is cause for an automatic rejection in most newspapers.
7. Do not hesitate to bring moral judgments to bear on the issue you are tackling. Appeal to the reader's sense of fair play, justice, and even mercy.

8. You can make a few language changes in your letter and, in that way, send it to editors of newspapers in other cities. You should change the language a little because many metropolitan newspapers (most notably the *New York Times*) will not publish a letter that has also been sent to other papers.

9. Always sign your name and give your address and phone number as the letter will, in all probability, be verified. You may use a pen name, but the editor must know the source of the letter.

10. Do not despair if your letter is not printed the same week it was mailed. And do not be utterly discouraged if it is never printed. At least the editor saw it and now has the benefit of your views on the topic. So— try again.

CORRESPONDING WITH GOVERNMENT OFFICIALS

Writing Tips

Rep. Morris K. Udall, (D. Ariz.) and the League of Women Voters have provided these suggestions on how to write to a member of Congress.

1. Write to your own senator or congressperson only. Letters written to others will eventually end up on the desk of your representative anyway.

2. Write at the proper time, when a bill is being discussed or on the floor.

3. Use your own words and your own stationery. Avoid signing and sending a form or mimeographed letter.

4. Do not be a pen pal; do not try to instruct the representative on every issue that arises.

5. Do not demand a commitment before all the facts are in. Bills rarely become law in the same form in which they are introduced.

6. Identify all bills by their title or their number.

7. If possible, include pertinent editorials from local newspapers.

8. Be constructive. If a bill deals with a problem that you admit exists, but you believe the bill is the wrong approach, tell what you think the right approach should be.

9. If you have expert knowledge or wide experience in a particular area, share it with the appropriate person. But do not pretend to wield vast political influence.

10. Write to a member of Congress when the legislator does something you approve of, too. A note of appreciation will make you be remembered more favorably the next time.

11. Feel free to write when you have a question or problem dealing with procedures of government departments.

12. Ask to be put on the mailing list for the newsletter. Most representatives today distribute newsletters and often send questionnaires soliciting constituents' opinions.

13. A telegram is an attention getter and is especially effective just before a vote. It is also easy to send. Just lift your phone and send a two-dollar, 15-word Public Opinion Message.
14. Finally, be brief, write legibly, and be sure to use the proper form of address.

Correct Form for Writing to Government Officials

President
The President
The White House
Washington, D.C. 20500

Dear Mr. President:
Very respectfully yours,

Vice-President
The Vice-President
The White House
Washington, D.C. 20500

Dear Mr. Vice-President:
Sincerely yours,

Senator
The Honorable [Full Name]
United States Senate
Washington, D.C. 20510

Dear Senator [Name]:
Sincerely yours,

Representative
The Honorable [Full Name]
House of Representatives
Washington, D.C. 20515

Dear Mr. or Ms. [Name]:
Sincerely yours,

Member of the Cabinet
The Honorable [Full Name]
The Secretary of the Treasury
Washington, D.C. 20520

Dear Mr. or Ms. Secretary:
Sincerely yours,

DEVELOPING A BOOK REPORT

Evaluating the Book

Usually the student is required to evaluate and report on books that have been assigned. The *date* of publication of a book may be very important. That is to say, *when* the book was written is the key to the *stage* of discussion of a given topic. For example, a book on moon topography published in the 1950s, before man visited the moon, would be of considerably less value than one written today. Also, the name of the *publisher* may offer some hint as to where the writer is from and what his biases and points of view are. Certain publishers specialize in books written from a certain viewpoint or champion certain schools of thought.

The author's *preface* or an *introduction* by a known authority will usually supply clues to the orientation and scope of the work. The *table of contents* offers further clues, as does a scanning of the *footnote-bibliography* sections. And just as important in this regard is the *index,* if there is one. For example, if a book entitled *Ancient Philosophies* contains many references to Plato and only a few to Aristotle, you may assume that the author has been more influenced by Plato than by Aristotle. Similarly, if the index holds many references to Christian writers, it is safe to assume that the author is viewing his topic from a Christian viewpoint.

If a book you will use as a source has been reviewed, by all means read the *reviews* before tackling the book. There are several reasons for this. First, the reviewer is professionally bound to have identified the main points; in addition, he probably will have noted the author's adherence to or departure from traditional approaches; finally, you may wish to cite the opinion(s) of the reviewer in your paper.

The more expert the researcher becomes in the general area of political science (and in dealing with intellectual materials in general), the more efficiently and instinctively he will be able to evaluate a book on politics. Nevertheless, for the tyro in political science research, there are various guidelines to help him or her decide the worth and reliability of a book. Foremost of these are the publisher and the author.

Is the publisher of the book in question reputable? The university presses usually publish material of a high academic quality, and the more prestigious the university, the more likely the book is to be authoritative. Then, too, certain series of books have a reputation for accuracy and reliability.

Now, what is the author's reputation? If it is strong in the field in which he or she is writing, then you most likely can relax with the conclusions drawn. But should the author be writing on politics from a dais or theater (e.g., Richard Burton on the pathology of politics), then the conclusions are at least suspect. For this reason, it is wise to consult *Who's Who in America,* or some similar reference, if the author is unknown to you. Beyond this, does the author's viewpoint, even in a field of expertise, affect the usefulness of the conclusions? It is vitally important to know the general position the author holds, especially in areas of controversy, for a political philosopher from the analytic, Anglo-Saxon school will approach a problem far differently than a political philosopher from the continental European school. Doctrinal and factional considerations may mean that a recognized authority in one of these traditions may be considered unhelpful in another.

For the student, all this can be bewildering. It is a difficult task to sort out the intrinsic value of the work. But when one becomes sufficiently competent, certain assumptions and approaches will be elevated, cataloged, or discarded. Until then, the neophyte in political science cannot afford the luxury of facile judgments but must consider all these legitimate and provisionally valuable.

Here are some specific ways to form a judgment about a book's value:
1. Read the table of contents and the index. What is suggested in the table of contents as the topic and approach of the work?

2. If there is a preface, does it pinpoint the scope and concerns of the author?
3. Does the index reflect an overbalance in one direction or another of any of several schools of thought on the topic?
4. Does the book deal with a field generally, or does it zero in on your research topic?
5. Is the author without prejudice, discussing opponents fairly and at length? Is the argument based on opinion or on fact? Is the logic of the argument sound? Are objections to the stated position considered? Does the author depend on reliable authorities? Do footnoting and bibliography seem appropriate? And finally, does the effectiveness of the presentation depend on literary charm rather than on the substantive aspects of information and argument?

Writing the Book Report

The following outline will help the student produce an acceptable paper.
1. Identify the work. Use proper bibliographical citation form (see pp. 119–23).
2. Classify the work, e.g., fiction, nonfiction, biography, general account, special account, monograph, periodical article, essay, proceedings, etc.
3. Identify the author(s). Give their background and qualifications for writing the work (unless obvious).
4. Outline the thesis (if any). What is the theme, special ''message,'' or point? Why has the author written this book this way? What is the purpose?
5. Note the organization. List the topics covered, scope of the work (or the selection), period covered, subjects omitted, factors not taken into account that influence the quality of the work. Has the author provided adequate maps, illustrative materials, etc.?
6. Check out the sources. Where has the author found the information? What kinds of sources are used—original manuscripts, monographs, secondary sources, interviews, etc.? Do you consider them adequate?
7. Note the amount read. List pages and chapters read or scanned, distinguishing between the two. (If you read the entire work, give the number of pages.)
8. Do a critical evaluation. In a page or two, indicate what stands out—your personal reaction to the body of the work.

A SHORTHAND SYSTEM FOR MARKING PERSONAL COPIES OF BOOKS

The authors firmly believe in marking up one's *own* books. A book is a research tool and can be made even more useful if it bears some record of impressions from previous readings. Consequently, a shorthand system may be suggested that quickly and neatly reminds the researcher of judgments of various materials in the book. This shorthand, or symbolic retrieval, system may include signs, symbols, numbers, or any device the researcher can easily recognize. The following are simply examples of what may be done. Your own system will undoubtedly be highly personalized:

1. *for important; **for very important
2. F for fact
3. T for theory
4. P for principle
5. ? for doubtful
6. S for suggestive
7. Cf. (compare) as in cf. Plato, *Republic II.*
8. Incl. for include in research paper
9. Q, or Par. for quote or paraphrase in the paper
10. X for the researcher not being sure of the value of the author's point

Such signs written in the margin of a book can and should be combined. E.g., *F means an important fact; ?PcfFord means a doubtful principle that is to be compared or contrasted to the Ford approach or principle in the same matter. This sort of shorthand may also be used in one's notebook to annotate class notes and then to glean quickly the material to be included in the research paper.

INTERVIEWING

There are two types of interviewing: elite interviewing and survey research. In elite interviewing, one questions a relatively small number of people who have a relatively large amount of information on a particular subject, e.g., a legislator or a mayor. Elites almost by definition are very busy people and are in a sense a perishable data source. If you are unprepared to ask intelligent questions, or if you ask questions that are easily answerable from public records, you might well find the interview abruptly cut short. Elite interviewing is an art involving a personal transaction between you and the interviewee. The best discussion of this sophisticated art is in Lewis Anthony Dexter, *Elite and Specialized Interviewing: Handbooks for Research in Political Behavior* (Evanston, Ill.: Northwestern University Press, 1970).

Some much more basic rules and techniques (mostly don'ts) are paraphrased from the American University Washington Semester Program instructions to undergraduate interviewers:

1. Try to make an appointment. Do not just "drop in" on a busy official unless he has invited you to do so, or unless you have been unable to get his office to give you an appointment.
2. Be prompt for appointments. Leave a sufficient safety margin in your travel time to the appointment to cover accidental delays and getting lost.

3. While waiting to be shown in, verify the spelling of the name and title of the official you are going to interview, and the pronunciation of his name, if in doubt. Write these things down for your bibliography and other later uses. Mark down the date of the interview.

4. Ask the secretary, also, for printed materials that might be available.

5. Begin the interview by telling briefly who you are, why you are doing the project, and what it is about.

6. Have several specific questions prepared, covering your purpose for being there. These should fill necessary gaps remaining in your information after you have done all the reading for the project. These questions may then lead to others.

7. Take notes only with permission, and even then, only if you are sure that doing so will not destroy the usefulness of the interview. Sometimes it is better to wait until the interview is over to take down what was said.

8. Do not quote one official to another!

9. Thank the person interviewed and leave just as soon as you feel that you have the information you need, unless he or she is clearly not busy and is willing to talk further. Don't overstay your welcome.

10. Write a note of thanks to the person interviewed within a week. This should be regarded as a strict obligation. No single act does more for the benefit of future students seeking similar interviews.

Remember that you are carrying the reputation of your college on your shoulders when interviewing. If you leave behind you a trail of irritation, or if you present yourself ill prepared, or if you fail to show decent courtesy and gratitude, you will make life that much harder for other students who may come later to interview the same people.

As a final note about interviewing, bear in mind that you are doing serious research. The number of interviews is far less important than the quality of the information gained. Seek out the knowledgeable, not the garrulous, and ask each interviewee for suggestions for future interviews.

Survey research, on the other hand, involves interviewing a representative sample of, for example, citizens or government workers on a matter in which they are not experts and might not even be interested. Their lack of knowledge or interest is itself data, and you will have to find a systematic way to record their nonresponse. Survey research thus involves selecting a representative sample from a larger population—and making this selection without biasing the results can be difficult.

The relatively large numbers of respondents and the possible low level of knowledge or interest means that a carefully constructed questionnaire with coded answers must also be devised. If elite interviewing as described by Dexter is an art, then survey research must resemble a science. One exposition of the intricacies of this form of scientific endeavor is Charles Backstrom and Gerald Hursh, *Survey Research* (Evanston, Ill.: Northwestern University Press, 1963).

OBSERVATION

There are certain kinds of information available only through firsthand observation. For instance, only by actually observing city council meetings could one capture the full debate, because in many cities there is only the most minimal public record or media coverage. Likewise, only by observing a local public health center could one find out how long individuals have to wait before they are treated. A significant variation of observation is experimentation—where the researchers themselves provide the stimuli for an observation. An example would be asking members of a council a pointed question at a public meeting. Such experimentation must be done more than once on a systematic basis to develop comparable data. There is no single source on observation and experimentation. The following is the best overall source:

Eugene Webb, et al, *Unobtrusive Measures: Non-Reactive Research in the Social Sciences* (Chicago: Rand McNally, 1966).

SHELF BROWSING

All libraries use one of the two subject classification systems described below. Once you locate the *several* areas where books on your subject are shelved, you can simply browse. Remember, however, to double-check the card catalog to identify the various subject headings.

The following explanation of library classification systems will help you locate the proper section.

Dewey Decimal Classification

Melvil Dewey worked out this approach in the latter part of the nineteenth century. The Dewey decimal classification system divides all knowledge, as represented by books and other materials that are acquired by libraries, into nine main classes, which are numbered by the digits 1 to 9. Material too general to belong to any one of these classes, such as newspapers and encyclopedias, falls into a tenth class, numbered 0, which precedes the others. The classes are written as hundreds; thus, 000 is general works, 100 is philosophy, 200 is religion, 300 is social sciences, and so on. Each division is subdivided into nine sections preceded by a general section; thus, 300 is the social sciences in general, while 321 is forms of state, 322 the state and religion, 323 the relationship between states and individuals or groups, etc. Further division to bring states and individuals or groups, etc. Further division to bring together like materials is accomplished by the addition of digits following a decimal point. Usually, most numbers do not exceed six digits in length, i.e., three to the right of the decimal point; however, there are cases of numbers extending to nine or more digits.

The basic classification system ranges from 000 to 999:

000–099	General works
100–199	Philosophy
200–299	Religion
300–399	Social sciences
400–499	Language
500–599	Pure sciences
600–699	Technology
700–799	Arts
800–899	Literature
900–999	History

The broad category of most relevance to political scientists is 300–399, the social sciences:

300–309	The social sciences, general
310–319	Statistics
320–329	Political science
330–339	Economics
340–349	Law
350–359	Public administration
360–369	Social welfare
370–379	Education
380–389	Public services and utilities
390–399	Customs and folklore

The specific category of most relevance to this study is that of "political science" (320–329), which is broken down into ten subclasses, each of which may be further subdivided by the use of decimals. For example, the subclass 326, "slavery," then becomes 326.1, "slave trade"; 326.2., "coolies and contract slaves"; 326.3, "serfs and serfdom"; and so forth:

320	Political science, general
321	Forms of states
322	State and church
323	State and individual
324	Suffrage and elections
325	Suffrage and elections
325	Migration and colonization
326	Slavery
327	Foreign relations
328	Legislation
329	Political parties

For the complete list of subclassifications, see the *Dewey Decimal Classification and Relative Index,* 18th ed., 2 vols. (New York: Forest Press, of Lake Placid Club Education Foundation, 1970).

Library of Congress Classification

The Library of Congress classification system was adopted in 1900, three years after the Library of Congress moved from the Capitol to its new building. The library changed systems to have a more systematic and functional arrangement of its collection. It is the system employed by most college libraries today.

This system divides the fields of knowledge into groups by assigning a letter to each and combining arabic numerals to separate the main groups into classes and subclasses in a way similar to that used in the Dewey decimal system. All books are divided into the following basic groups:

A	General works	M	Music
B	Philosophy and religion	N	Fine arts
C	History and auxiliary sciences	P	Language and literature
		Q	Science
D	Foreign history and topography	R	Medicine
		S	Agriculture
E–F	American history	T	Technology
G	Geography and anthropology	U	Military science
H	Social science	V	Naval science
J	Political science	Z	Bibliography and library science
K	Law		
L	Education		

For political scientists, class J (political science) is the most relevant. Within each class, subdivisions are denoted by a second letter. Thus for political science, we have the following subclasses:

J	Official documents
JA	General works
JC	Political theory
JF	Constitutional history and administration
JK	United States
JL	British America, Latin America
JN	Europe
JQ	Asia, Africa, Australia, Pacific Island
JS	Local government
JV	Colonies and colonization
JX	International law and international relations

Each subclass makes up several smaller regional, historical, or functional subdivisions. For the complete list of subclassifications see *Classification: Class J, Political Science,* 2d ed. (Washington, D.C.: Government Printing Office, 1924; reprinted in 1966).

Index